WHERE THE SIX MILE WATER FLOWS

This book is dedicated to the memory of the late Bertie Scott from Ballylinney whose lively wit and amusing anecdotes delighted the many friends he made during a lifetime spent farming in the Six Mile valley.

The publication has received support from the Cultural Traditions Group of the Community Relations Council

The Friar's Bush Press
24 College Park Avenue
Belfast BT7 1LR
1991
© Copyright reserved
ISBN 0 9846872 44 9

Front Cover: The Lynn burn just before it enters the Six Mile Water at the Ballyclare paper mill (McKeown Coll.)

Designed by Leslie Stannage Design, Belfast
Printed by W. & G. Baird, Antrim

WHERE THE *Six Mile Water* FLOWS

Historic photographs of the Ballyclare area, Co. Antrim

From the scree slopes up above on Shane's dark brooding hill
To the little wandering stream below where cattle drink their fill
Here springs the lovely Ollar, once known as Owen-na view
But is now the Six Mile Water, banks glistening in the dew.

Ernest McA. Scott

JACK McKINNEY

FRIAR'S BUSH PRESS

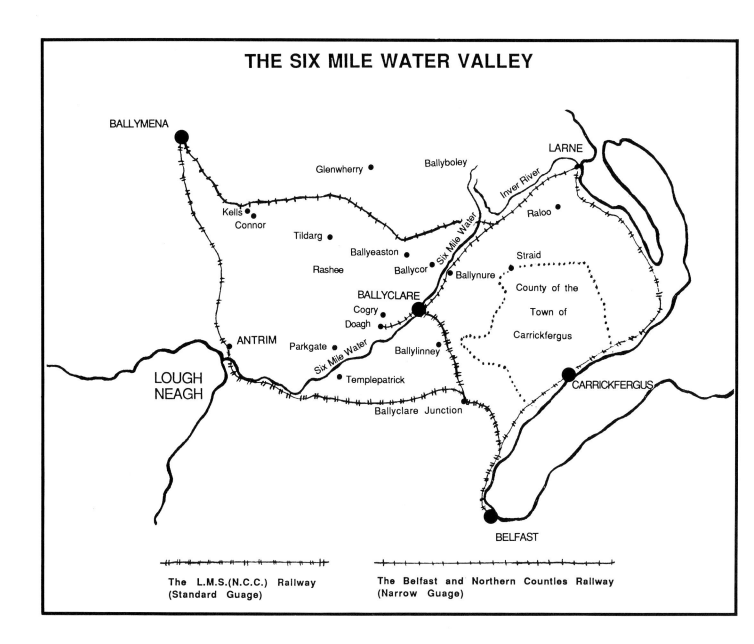

THE SIX MILE WATER VALLEY

BALLYMENA

Glenwherry •

Ballyboley

LARNE

Kells •
Connor •

Inver River

Raloo •

Tildarg •

Ballyeaston •

Six Mile Water

Straid •

Rashee

Ballycor •

County of the

BALLYCLARE

Ballynure •

Town of

Cogry •
Doagh •

Carrickfergus

ANTRIM

Parkgate •

Six Mile Water

Ballylinney

CARRICKFERGUS

LOUGH
NEAGH

• Templepatrick

Ballyclare Junction

BELFAST

The L.M.S.(N.C.C.) Railway
(Standard Guage)

The Belfast and Northern Counties Railway
(Narrow Guage)

THE SIX MILE RIVER VALLEY

The Six Mile Water, or Ollar or Owen-na-view, the names by which the river has been known in the past, rises in the Park Moss, Ballyboley. But it is only when the many small streams meet near Ballynure and begin to meander westwards towards Lough Neagh that its true course really begins. This book also starts in this pleasant village and finds stopping points, if not always beside the river then at least not far from its banks.

The beauty of the Six Mile Water valley has been enjoyed and its fertility exploited for centuries by successive waves of settlers making their way up river from the coast. The landscape they saw was certainly spectacular. In a description of Co. Antrim in 1812 Rev. John Dubordieu put it rather well.

In the openings of these mountains to the west are some vallies of considerable extent and great fertility. That of the Six Mile Water, which contains the villages of Straid, Ballynure, Ballyeaston, Doagh and Templepatrick, is a fine specimen of the beauty and cultivation of the county, to which the frequent white-thorn hedges contribute not a little, shewing as the plains about Antrim are approached, the increasing richness of the soil by their superior size and vigour.

However, the river had its disadvantages. Flooding was once a dangerous seasonal hazard. It is significant that the origin of the name "Ollar" referred to the stretches of tall rushes so common along its marshy banks, especially east of Ballyclare. Fortunately nowadays flood damage has been minimised by drainage schemes and deaths rarely occur. It wasn't always so. *The Northern Star* in March 1795 starkly reported how Surgeon Bell of Ballyclare on his return from Ballytweedy missed his way at the turn into the Templepatrick Road and, riding straight on, was lost in the Six Mile Water.

When Carrickfergus was the garrison and county town, soldiers would have been a common sight riding to Antrim along the valley. Their route from Carrick first crossed a stream called the Three Mile Water and then eventually struck The Six Mile Water which they followed to Antrim. The Ollar then came to be known as The Six Mile Water, the soldier's contact being that distance in Irish miles from their garrison town.

Life in this pleasant valley has always been firmly centred on farming and the textile industry. Both activities depended upon the rich soil and an abundance of water. The main river and its fast descending tributaries consistently provided enough water for crops and the generation of power.

Of all the settlements in the valley, Ballyclare eventually became the most important as a centre of markets and industry. Its natural advantage was a reliable stony ford capable of use throughout the year. Later, the age of steam brought two railways to Ballyclare, and easy acess to regular supplies of coal for industry, from the nearby port of Larne. Thus the town expanded spectacularly in the late 19th and early 20th centuries, its new population coming from the surrounding villages. It is therefore not surprising that in a book about the Six Mile valley most of the text and photographs should concentrate on the central market town. The surrounding villages each make a unique contribution to the general picture of life in the area, and an attempt has been made to include material interesting and typical of each village.

Town and village have in common the nature and ancestry of the people. The surnames so familiar in the area - Wilson, Kennedy, Houston, Blair, McClean, and the distinct dialect clearly show the Scottish origin of the settlers. Their traditional respect for hard work is tempered by an obvious enjoyment of wit and humour while their support in the past for radical causes such as the Hearts of Steel land reform movement and the 1798 rebellion stems from their strong non-conformist roots. This book dwells less on such momentous incidents than on the personalities and social occasions which have contributed so much colour to life in Ballyclare and the villages of this beautiful river valley since the end of last century. Its splendour is nowhere more fervently described than in a piece from a programme for a bazaar in Ballyclare Presbyterian Church in 1899:

Looking down the valley from the summit of the surrounding hills a panaroma lies unfolded before us which is a perfect feast to the eye. The serpentine course of the river as it ripples on towards Lough Neagh seems like a thread of silver running through a fabric of emerald, and the graceful, verdant slopes, wooded here and there down to the water's edge, make up a landscape unsurpassed for its beauty in the whole province of Ulster.

BALLYNURE

It could justly be claimed that at one time Ballynure was a place of greater importance than Ballyclare. Interestingly one boundary of the parish of Ballynure is at the Six Mile Water bridge in Ballyclare. Part of Ballyclare is therefore in Ballynure! The population of the village used to be much larger than it is today. In the last century and earlier there was an extensive rural hinterland with many people who looked to Ballynure for the services of its tradesmen and markets. In the last century the village could support four pubs and, perhaps consequently, a police barracks with four constables. Even then it was necessary sometimes to call in soldiers to keep the peace. Below the site of the presbyterian church there were once twenty workers' houses and nearby in quaintly named Graveyard Row there were many more, mostly for employees of the cotton mill.

Like Straid, the village has always looked more to Carrickfergus than Ballyclare. The major landowner for centuries has been the Dobbs family and this ensured Ballynure's close connection with the county town.

The name means 'the townland of the yew tree' and its twin claims to popular fame are usually quoted as its connection with the cleric Dean Swift, who preached in the old church at Ballynure, and as the spot mentioned in the fine traditional song 'The Ballad of Ballynure'.

In the 19th century, Ballynure had a large, four-storied cotton mill with 9000 spinning mules in operation at its peak. Its impressive size can be judged from the extensive ruins of the three stories still standing. Robert Howe developed this business from an old corn mill on this site. In 1832 he also excavated a dam at Straid linked by sluices and channels to Ballynure. This supplemented the water flow from the Six Mile Water and the small tributaries which converge near the village. The mill complex was never converted to steam so, inevitably, declined.

Its closure in the 1860s was caused by the combined effects of the American Civil War on the supplies of raw cotton and a tragic accident which happened to the son of Robert Howe its owner. He was killed in September 1851 when the floor collapsed in the loft of the old paper mill in Ballyclare where he had been attending a performance given by a hypnotist. There was a beetling mill on the site, too, working up to 1899, but eventually the premises were taken over by Mc Kerrells, manufacturors of farm machinery, especially reapers and barn threshers, some of which still survive today. A part of the old mill was formerly used as a store for bauxite from the Straid mines, before the ore was taken to the Ballynure railway station nearby.

Just off the street in Ballynure, at one time there was a piece of common land called 'The Shilling Hill'. Here locals could graze donkeys, goats, pigs or fowl. When, controversially, the land was enclosed one annoyed user, Alec Leech, is said to have complained bitterly, 'There's no more grass for Leech's ass upon the Shilling Hill'.

In the 18th century, the highly respected weaver poet, James Campbell, lived near Ballynure and in 1797 the body of William Orr, the famous radical, was waked in the presbyterian church after he was hanged in Carrickfergus. At the turn of the century Billy Girvan owned an extensive drapery, grocery, general store and posting establishment in the village. His son, Thomas, extended the service until his fine, horse-drawn coach, 'The Ballynure Flyer', with glass windows and solid sides capable of carrying 32 passengers, made the journey to Belfast four times each week. Later the Girvan family moved their business to Ballyclare and from here their motor vehicles took tourists all round Ulster.

Today Ballynure is bypassed and the vehicles on the main Belfast - Larne trunk road whizz noisily past just yards from the village. Perhaps the bustle occasionally reminds older residents of the journeys on the Ballynure Flyer. Its sad fate was to end up as a hen house in a nearby field where its remains could be seen until quite recently.

BLACKSMITH AT WORK IN BALLYNURE, *c.*1920

In former times the village blacksmith was a very important person because he made the tools for other tradesmen but, more recently, shoeing horses and making and repairing farm machinery was their main employment. Here a member of the Barr family, long associated with the trade in Ballynure, practises his craft with the usual quota of spectators. The cottages on the right and John McKinstry's little shop have since been demolished but the exterior of Hill's detached house has changed little. This whole area was altered in the 1950s when the Larne to Belfast trunk road was re-aligned and the village by passed. The view, indeed, is seen roughly from the position of the new road. (G. McKeown Coll.)

SKILGANABAN P. E. SCHOOL GROUP, 1930

The townland of Skilganaban is on the southern bank of the Six Mile Water mid-way between Ballynure and Ballyclare. There was a school here since 1825 but it closed in 1933 when a new extension to the old National School buildings, opened at Ballyclare two miles away. The pupils were drawn either from this farming area or Millvale a cluster of houses near the old paper mill. The teachers are Mr Gillen and Miss Patton. The group contains many brothers and sisters whose family names - Kennedy, Woodside, Logan, Brennan, Blair, Wallace and Rutherford - have always been very prevalent in this district. (Mrs W. Mairs Coll.)

BALLYNURE BEETLING MILL, *c.*1926

This mill was situated on the Castle Road, where the houses of Castletown Park have since been built. It had a large, 28 foot, water wheel and was originally owned by the Girvan family from Ballynure. The water came to the wheel from Straid dam by a layde and then via the wooden trough, seen above at the left gable of the mill. The beetling machinery, which added a shine to linen cloth, was in the bottom storey, the others being used for storage. At one time a saw mill was operated along with the beetling. The mill lay idle for many years before Kirkpatrick's Bros, the bleachers in Ballyclare, took it over to help them cope with a boom in their textile trade. It closed in the late 1930s, and machinery and contents were sold off for scrap. (E. Scott Coll.)

5

STRAID

Straid, formerly known as Thomas Town, lies three miles from Ballyclare but like its neighbour Ballynure, has many associations with Carrickfergus. Not far east of the village are to be found the Irish and Scotch Hills, the Quarterlands and the Commons of Carrickfergus. Near the village the Watch Hill where, in the 16th century the veteran garrison regiment, the Fogies, looked for the approach of the McDonnells from the Glens, is near the village. Straid was on the boundary of the Town and County of Carrickfergus and the Dobbs estate property. In the 18th century the Mayor of Carrickfergus had to ride around the county boundary each year and when he came along the Ballylagan road from Raloo to Straid it was his custom to take a claret cup sitting on his horse in the garden of the mansion house. This was simply a large residence in the main street and was the property of the Ellis family of Carrickfergus.

Water has always been important to Straid and its dam, now a thriving trout fishery, was excavated in 1832 by John Howe at the same time as he built the cotton mill in Ballynure. An elaborate system of laydes and sluices carried the water from Straid to the mill and indeed a century later this water was still being used by Kirkpatrick Brothers' bleaching works, having been diverted to their Ballyclare factory.

In 1875 bauxite ore was discovered on the hill just above the village and mining of the mineral gradually increased until its peak during the First World War. This provided useful employment not just in the mines but for many farmers who were contracted to transport the ore to the narrow gauge railway station at Ballynure. Fortunately this journey was almost all downhill and the large farm carts used could take one ton per load, needing trace horses only on a short hilly stretch outside the village.

It is not generally known that Straid Plantin', a well known landmark, was originally intended as timber for pit props in the mines. They ceased operation just after the Second World War but the water from the deep mines continued to be piped to the village pumps. Indeed Irish Hill water is now being bottled commercially for the flourishing spring water market. One relic of the mining operation is the remains of the old pumping station still to be seen close to the depression in the road known as the 'Dippa', between Straid and Mossley.

There was also a corn mill near the village, owned by the Wilson family, a name always very common in Straid. This bruised grain for farmers, while a flax mill reputed to be one of the oldest in area, was also situated nearby and still has some of the scutching machines in place.

Like all country villages Straid has had its share of personalities over the years. Many older folk may fondly remember "Cuddy Fud" an old woman who went from door to door selling baps and black balls, or in a later period Johnny Cowden, a butcher who killed his own animals and travelled round the district selling his meat from a basket. Straid's hero, though, was undoubtedly John E. Furniss, son of the manager of the bauxite mines, who was one of the 'First Hundred' from the Ballyclare area in 1914 to enlist for action in the First World War. Earlier that year, indeed, he had played a prominent part in the famous U.V.F. gun-running escapade at Larne and he had hidden a large quantity of illegal rifles and ammunition in the depths of the bauxite mines. He rapidly rose through the ranks and eventually became an army captain. He was respected for conspicuous bravery especially by daring raids into 'no-man's land' and was eventually wounded in action on one escapade when a Ballyclare comrade remarked, "Furniss was fighting mad, I believe that if he hadn't been wounded he would have been in Berlin that night taking us all with him." The valour of Jack Furniss was recognised when he became the first officer of the 108th Military Brigade to be decorated for bravery. He was awarded the Military Cross and survived to return to Straid as a popular hero after the war.

THE VILLAGE OF STRAID IN THE LATE 1930s

Today the village retains much of the serenity of this photograph but, recently, the large tree, a feature of Straid for many years, has had to be truncated. Just beyond it was a shop for general provisions, belonging to the Wilson family who have been in business here for many generations. It served a very wide area around the village and remains open to the present day. The lady on the pavement has been identified as a Mrs McClean from the village. (J. Boyd Coll.)

BALLYEASTON

The village of Ballyeaston is situated on a hill overlooking the Six Mile river, and the First Presbyterian Church, standing on a prominence in the village reminds one of an acropolis. Churches, if not temples, have always dominated Ballyeaston. Its very name is a corruption of Austin or Augustine's town, the original church being dedicated to this saint. This was one of four churches founded in this area by St Patrick, the others being at Ballycorr, less than a mile to the east, Rashee, the same distance to the west, and Ballynure. Each had a holy well and the one at Ballyeaston was closed up only about forty years ago. Older villagers would have drawn water from it. The ruins of the ancient parish church, still standing are of a building erected in 1786 and closed on Easter Day, 1894, when a new parish was centred in Ballyclare. Some of the slates of the old building were used in St John's, when it was built on the Doagh Road, Ballyclare in 1904. Today there are two presbyterian churches in a village of around 200 people. The First Church was founded in 1676 and the Second, a seceding congregation, moved here from the Five Corners, Rashee, over 170 years ago. The first minister of the Ballyeaston congregation, Rev. William Adair, had the distinction of being one of the deputation which met King William at Carrickfergus in 1690.

Ballyeaston had strong connections with the 1798 Rebellion and even here there was a church connection. The clergyman of the Second congregation actually drilled volunteers in a field next to his manse. Since then these have been known as the 'parade field' and 'parade manse'. The leader of the local brigade was Alec Hay, a store keeper in the village, and after its failure he surrendered to the Crown forces saving the village from annihilation at the expense of his life. He was hanged at Carrickfergus.

In 1801 the parish of Ballyeaston was extensive, its population numbered 5982, but like the village, gradually declined during this century. In 1841 the village had 265 people but in 1891 only 159. Similarly the townland, a much smaller area than the parish, dropped from 390 in 1841 to 174 in 1891. Because of the populous hinterland Ballyeaston, not surprisingly, could support a large school in 1840. Indeed two schools, one male with two rooms, and a female school also with two rooms operated in the same large building. Ballyeaston was first in the district to have a separate school for girls, a very progressive idea at this time.

The village at one time had a tan yard, possibly an iron works, nine houses where liquor could be bought and, no doubt as a consequence of this trade, its own police barracks. There were many weavers in the village and vicinity but later in the 19th century the main employment in the area was at the Whitepark bleaching works just below the village on the Six Mile Water. Indeed a right of way still exists down to the works.

Ballyeaston is a pleasant place in which to live and, evidently, it was a healthy area too. In the *Belfast News Letter* of April 7, 1739, it is reported that a John Magrady, of the Parish of Ballyeaston, Ballyclare was then 113 years old and had never been affected by any sickness although he had not washed his hands or face for 30 years nor combed his head for 40 years. He had married four years previously a woman aged between 30–40 years. It is hard to say whether this achievement is more a reflection of the strength of the men in Ballyeaston, or the desperation of the women in this Six Mile Water village.

THE HOLY WELL AT BALLYEASTON, EARLY 1900s
This rare though well known photograph is of the Holy Well associated with the ancient church, St Augustine's, in Ballyeaston. In keeping with the presbyterian tradition it was never kept sacred and apart, in modern times at least, but was used for domestic supplies until a mains water supply reached the village in the 1930s. It was damaged during some work associated with the installation of a sewerage scheme and filled in. Now covered over, the site is unmarked in the car park beside the 2nd Presbyterian Congregation's church hall. The woman in the picture is reliably thought to be from the Allan family. A relation of hers presently resides in the village main street. (Dr R. Millar Coll.)

BALLYEASTON FLUTE BAND AND
ORANGE LODGE, 12th JULY 1923

The village band and lodge are seen here before setting off for 'the field'. The band was formed in 1892 and in 1923 shared a hall with the lodge, the building to the left in the photograph. In the mid 1930s a new Orange Hall was built on the road to Ballyclare and the old hall was sold to the band. This band was very successful in championships until its demise in 1965. The bandroom still exists, with a commemorative plaque on its outside wall. It is now unoccupied and held in trusteeship. Many Ballyeaston folk can be recognised here including the Millar brothers, Bob and Johnny, prominent in the front row wearing soft hats. Bob was a well known tailor for many years in Ballyclare. (G. McKeown, T. Allan Coll.)

10

BALLYLINNEY

Ballylinney, 'the townland of the waterfall', is two miles south of Ballyclare. The Lynn Burn runs into the Six Mile Water at the paper mill and the beautiful glen, in which the waterfall is to be found, used to be a popular destination for walkers from Ballyclare. There was also a starch mill here but it ceased operation in 1847, probably due to the potato famine and the consequent shortage of potatoes from which the starch was obtained. The foundations of the ancient church, already decayed in 1622, remain in the old graveyard a field length below the present presbyterian church. This graveyard is unusual in being still administered by a committee of representatives from local families who, by tradition, meet each Easter to discuss interment rights and the care of the graves. The parish of Ballylinney three centuries ago was the property of the old Norman family, the de Logans, but they fared badly in the Earl of Tyrone's rising in 1641 when their base in Ballyclare was destroyed.

The Lynn Burn at Ballylinney. A figure can be seen beside the ruins of the old starch mill. (G. McKeown)

BUSINESS AND TRADE IN BALLYCLARE

As traffic across the ford in Ballyclare developed, naturally commerce increased. The first record of the importance of trade on the site seems to be in 1718 when the Carrickfergus agent of the Marquis of Donegall, a substantial landowner in this area, offered his lordship this advice about Ballyclare:

It is a very convenient place for tradesmen such as coopers, taylors, weavors, or shoomakers to live upon. . . I will use my utmost endeavour to erect what tenements you shall think convenient. . . and. . . to set them to good tenants and at the highest rent can be procured for them.

The boundary of the Donegall property was the river, and Ballyclare has always suffered a division because of this. The landlord south of the river, actually in the parish of Ballynure, had not the misfortune, like the Donegalls, to go bankrupt and sell out leases to tenants on attractive terms. The property in 'Le Ballyclare', or 'the fit o' the toon', as the area was colloquially known, was held insecurely on short leases in the past, and this has led to the persistence of small shop units here even up to the present day. Above the river, towards the 'heid o' the toon', the tenants had reasonable tenure. Their prosperity was reflected in their larger, more attractive establishments. Thus the two main business areas have always been Main Street and Market Square or Fair Green as it used to be called.

By 1891 the population had increased to 1600 and it surged to 3367 by 1926. A Bazaar brochure of 1899 lists some of the local businesses:

Watchmaking, Bootmaking, Bookmaking (a flourishing printer), Harnessmaking, Baking, Tailoring, Dressmaking, Embroidering, Coopering, Beetling, Farrying, Nailmaking, House Decorating and Painting, Plastering, Building, Coachbuilding, Furnituremaking.

There is quite a host of fine drapery establishments, several extensive grocery and hardware houses, two Hotels and a number of spirit retailers, boot shops, jeweller shops, druggists, fruiterers, and a Postal Telegraph Office and Savings Bank."

Many of the tradespeople in Ballyclare at this time were itinerant for part of the year. Travelling watch and clock makers with their little leather bag of tools and others peddled a variety of goods through the countryside. There were some distinctive characters who made their mark on the street. Charlie Cole, in a small thatched cottage on Main Street made, by hand, wire nails of every description for carpenters, slaters, blacksmiths and cobblers. His 'oiled ovals' were, on his word, the best in the land. Bella Price's small shop on Main Street supplied delicious lemonade, custard tarts, buns and gravy rings. Then, early this century, Fanny Cannon had a popular toy shop on the site where her father had earlier produced and sold leather goods. There was the cobbler, William Crawford, known as 'The Clogger', and Willie Rea and Robert Wilson who were more recent, skilled boot makers. A Dr Cunningham on Main Street, for some time combined the unusual roles of doctor and postmaster. Samuel Milliken and Henry Service were undertakers and transport operators before W.S. McConnell took over this business in the 1920s. Robert Grange reports how last century an individual transport entrepreneur operated a regular parcel service to Belfast in a wheelbarrow. Many lodging houses catered for "gentlemen and women of the road" and Jimmy Proctor and Sally McHurley (before a savage occupant slit her throat) kept their 'guests' in order and on the move.

However, in this town of eccentrics, one tradesman can not easily be forgotten. James Walmsley was a seedsman at the end of last century in a small cottage in the Square and, when business was slack, he used to disappear beneath the counter for forty winks on a bed kept there for this purpose.

Today, business in Ballyclare is once again booming, the shops obviously benefitting from the extensive housing developments springing up in the town and the surrounding villages. The branches of large chain stores, estate and insurance agencies operating in the town and the vast range of smaller enterprises, though obviously much more efficient, do lack something of the unorthodox character of their predecessors in this ever busy market town.

LOWER MAIN STREET, BALLYCLARE, *c*.1910

On the left, Baird's public house is having its supplies replenished. The ornate plaster work was a special feature of this attractive building. The large oil lamp on the corner was removed in the 1950s to allow easier access for tall vehicles, especially double decked buses, into Main Street. The entire pub was demolished in the 1960s. Samuel MisKimmin, historian of Carrickfergus, was born in a cottage on the site two premises up the street from Baird's. On the opposite side a large tree overhangs the street outside Ollar Lodge, formerly Ballyclare's courthouse. Behind it, and the row of premises on the right was the lock-up hardly big enough to warrant the term jail. On May Fair nights it was bulging. (G. McKeown Coll.)

13

MAIN STREET, LOOKING NORTH TO THE SQUARE, 1908

In the early 19th century Main Street was mainly residential but by 1908 this had become a prosperous, business area. The roads were not yet metalled but the Urban Council, formed in 1905, had the street soaked by a water cart in the summer to keep down the dust, known locally as 'stoor'. The zealous driver, Will Williamson, even operated on wet days! By contrast,

Charlie Cole's small thatched cottage, reflects the undeveloped nature of the right hand side of the street. The building directly above Cunningham's monogram on the right, next door to Cole's, is the house used by the sexton of the nearby Old Presbyterian Church. The church bell was formerly on the gable of this house. (J. Cunningham)

14

BALLYEASTON ROAD, BALLYCLARE, *c*.1910

This row of houses, probably built in the late 1800s is easily recognisable today by the peculiarly shaped gable end seen here on the right side of the photograph. Although external features have been altered they are essentially still the same structure. The row is a few yards beyond the junction with the route to Ballycorr, known at this time as the Whitepark Road. These new houses were a reflection of the commercial and industrial development of the town at this time. The waste patch in the foreground was built up soon after this date. (G.McKeown Coll.)

THE SQUARE LOOKING SOUTH WITH MARKET HOUSE, *c.*1910

In the mid 19th century a major redevelopment took place in the Square when a row of new premises was built in front of an old cow path to the river. The main purpose of the Square, however, remained as the site of markets and fairs until motor traffic forced animal sales on to an enclosed market yard nearby. On the right is the public weighbridge, beside the pigs' weighing area in the Market House. This was later to serve as a public library for a time. 'Fractions School' is on the far left. Its plaque can be clearly distinguished. The school had long since closed and the building served as a council room at this time, a contrast to the grandeur of the chamber in the present Town Hall. The baker's cart is a reminder that Ballyclare then had a depot for the distribution, but not the baking, of Inglis' bread. (G. McKeown Coll.)

16

THE MARKET SQUARE WITH THE CUNNINGHAM MONUMENT, *c.*1910

The monument was erected in 1854 to the memory of Dr James Cunningham, a local doctor, but was demolished in 1951 to help the problem of increasing motor traffic, especially buses, in the square. The monument was always a landmark in the market, and around it the fowl were noisily bartered. Here, too, farmers and prospective hired labourers would haggle on fair days. Before demolition the Ballyclare Council agreed to have the two relief placques on the base preserved and erected in the Town Hall lobby. This was not done and the placques were unaccountably lost. (Mrs R. Nelson Coll.)

17

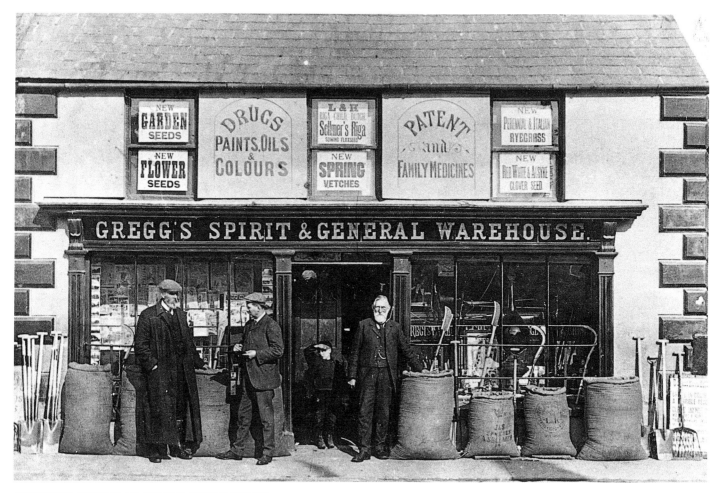

GREGG'S GENERAL STORE, THE LOWER
SQUARE, *c.*1912

James Gregg stands proudly outside his premises on the corner of the square. They extended right back along adjoining Park Street and sold hardware, animal foodstuffs, drugs, newspapers, groceries, fishing tackle, and guns and ammunition. There was a public bar and a fully equipped billiards room in behind the main store. The shop was famous for having a cockatoo which implored visitors, in a loud call to "scratch Cockey". Its owner, inevitably in a town addicted to nicknames, was known as Cockey Gregg. (R. T. Grange Coll.)

SAM HUSTON'S SADDLERY, *c.*1920s

This was one of many businesses in Ballyclare dealing with horse harness and other leather goods for farmers and hauliers over the years. These were made on the premises, near the square and on the corner of Park Street. At one time, the shop had a window looking on to this street and from this viewpoint or his front doorway Sam Houston could cast an experienced eye over the horses passing by or being shown in the street outside or in the square on market and fair days. (R. T. Grange Coll.)

FAIRS AND MARKETS

Markets and fairs have been held on various sites in the Six Mile valley for many generations. At one time it seems that almost every village of any size could boast a decent fair day. Eventually, however, Ballyclare completely dominated the local market and fair scene in the valley.

A map of Ballyclare in 1722 identifies a common, roughly equivalent to the traditional two acre market square, in use as a fair ground. Then in 1756 George the Second in a deed of grant saw fit to grant Arthur Earl of Donegall, *"two fairs yearly at the Town and lands of Ballyclare, also a weekly market to be held at the town aforesaid on every Wednesday for ever—also a Court of Pye Poudre to be held in the said town during the said fairs and markets"*

In the early years, linen was the most valuable product to be marketed in Ballyclare. This eventually declined but the weekly market generally prospered.

The Ordnance Survey Memoir of 1839 describes the general market.

The chief articles exposed for sale at the markets in Ballyclare are pigs, cows (a few) yarn, sheep, coopers vessels of wood, baskets, all brands of soft goods and hardware, delph and crockery, dulse, gingerbread, cheese, fruit in season and wool hats.

By contrast the seasonal fairs took place in and around the square and on the streets with no official organisation. Indeed it appears that they often attracted considerable opposition from the townsfolk and market committee. Considering what often took place in Ballyclare on market days this attitude is hardly surprising. By tradition they were held four times each year - in January, May, July and November, but it was always the May Fair which attracted most business and amusement activities, and it survived when the others ceased. From very early times the importance of the trade in horses at Ballyclare is very evident. Dubordieu commenting in 1812 on the markets and fairs in Co Antrim states:

Of these markets or fairs, Ballyclare seems to be the greatest resort of the dealers, the farmers in that neighbourhood being accounted very good judges of horses and the art of making up for sale.

Although all types of horses were on view there was always a very large proportion of the very best, young beasts. These found a ready market from dealers supplying good quality draught animals for work in cities in Britain. Also agents of foreign governments attended regularly to purchase mounts for cavalry regiments or heavy draught horses for gun carriages and the like. In November, and especially at the May Fair, there was a steady business in the hiring of labourers for the forthcoming season on farms in the district. Fairs and markets fulfil an important social function for farmers and other local people. The fairs, especially, were popular for the opportunities they afforded for enjoyment and indulgence alongside much essential business. The "goings-on" took a variety of forms but order and restraint were not often their most pleasing characteristics. Nor were they ever noted for temperance, with prodigious quantities of alcohol being consumed. Inevitably in the evening, but often much earlier, fierce battles raged at random throughout the town. Many were "faction fights" where clans or families settled old scores. Archibald McIlroy in the 1890s describes what an earlier writer had colourfully, but I'm sure, accurately termed a "rigorous tumult".

Looking down on the Fair Hill from the vicinity of the upper pump, a hundred ash sticks could be seen doing nasty work. Men were being dragged out from the thick of the fight whose features were hardly discernible through blood and bruises. Curses and fiendish yells rent the air and above all were the screams of the women in their wild efforts to save loved ones or, it must be confessed in some cases, to urge on the combatants.

Later, in this century, the May Fair developed into a popular carnival with the emphasis shifting decidedly from business to pleasure. There were many popular mechanical amusement rides but, as always, a few rather dubious games of chance defied official disapproval. But the best time for pure peace in Ballyclare was the week after the indulgences of the May Fair, even though local tradesmen found considerable difficulty when presenting their accounts.

The May Fair carnival week, after a lapse during the civil disturbances of the 1970s survives today and is as popular as ever with the usual crowds pouring into the town from the entire Six Mile Valley to enjoy the amusements.

TESTING WIND AND LIMB AT BALLYCLARE, 1927
The tradition of galloping a horse down the street at full pelt
much to the consternation yet enjoyment of crowds of
spectators goes back as far as the fairs themselves. Many
attempts, all hopelessly futile, have been made to end the
dangerous practice, but even today each May brings the
gallopers on to the busy street. (*Larne Times*)

THE MARKET HOUSE AND TOWN HALL, *c.*1910

A wooden market house was erected in the 18th century and then around 1866, a substantial stone market house was constructed. In 1873 an upper storey was added for use as a town hall. Eventually, in 1935 a large extension, including an impressive clock tower, gave the building its present profile.

The old clock can be seen just below the peak of the roof with the weather vane above. The round arched central opening is the entrance to the pork weighing room. A cart may be seen backing up to the doorway. (J. Cunningham)

MARKET DAY IN THE SQUARE, *c.*1890
In the centre Alex McGladdery, the well-known owner of the Farmers' Inn beside the Square monument is talking to a constable, with the tall buildings of Shannon's Row at the head of the square in the background. As a member of the Town Hall and Market committees he would have had a particular interest in the running of these important weekly markets. He was the last surviving member of the Market House Trust when in 1925, the building passed into the control of the Urban Council officially allowing their meetings to be held here.
(J. Cunningham)

PIG MARKET IN SQUARE, LOOKING TOWARDS
NORTH END, *c.*1890s

As opposed to dead pigs which were weighed at the Market House and sold as pork to dealers, young, live pigs in litters, were displayed and sold here from upended carts. This was an important market for many years and by tradition the carts lined up along the 'Trinket', an open drain which, with a hedge, had originally marked a route from Main Street through the Fair Green and thence to Doagh. The building right next to the three storied row, was where Fleming's shop was located in the 1950s before it was demolished. Except for the enclosure of the square, the appearance of this area has seen little structural change in the last hundred years. (R.T. Grange Coll.)

HORSE FAIR IN MAIN STREET, MAY 1907

This has always been the widest section of Main Street, and even today at the May Fair it still attracts the horses and donkeys. The photographer's own house is just beyond the 'cycles' sign. The gentleman in the right foreground can easily be identifed as Tom Calvert, a local pharmacist. The Thatch Inn is on the left and just above is Eliza (Granny) Moore's little cottage, the very last such home left on Main Street, and soon to be literally squeezed out of existence. (J. Cunningham)

THE MAY FAIR, 1890s (opposite) (G. McKeown Coll.)
AND 1929 (above) (*Larne Times*)

Every kind of amusement could be found in the square. Mechanical rides competed with the attractions of the gypsy fortune tellers, ballad singers, quack doctors and those selling ginger bread, yellow man and dulse. There were harness salesmen and dealers in toys and religious literature side-by-side with the illicit operators of roulette tables. Shifty fellows with crown and anchor boards mixed with other chancers who hoped to beguile their country clients with the famous 'Find-the-lady' card trick. And everywhere there were the pickpockets reaping a rich harvest and hoping to avoid a visit to the busy courthouse next day.

27

INDUSTRY

Agriculture has always been the main occupation of the people of the Six Mile valley but an extensive range of other important industries have flourished from time to time. The connection, from the earliest times, between farming and other manufacturing and service industries has been significant. The textile industry is a good example. The linen finishing trade began in Ballyclare with the manufacture of muslin for butter making on farms. In the past, the cultivation of flax was followed by spinning and weaving done on the farms, by the families themselves or by itinerant tradesmen. Then, with the eventual harnessing of water and then steam power to these processes in the 19th century, the scale and economics of such enterprises demanded a separate and specialist operation although the many bleach greens in the area dating from the 17th century point to early specialisation. By 1780, Lendrick's map shows three bleach greens in the Parish of Kilbride alone. These provided scope for entrepreneurs to develop a valuable business and many local families became wealthy through this trade.

The coming of steam to the area changed the pattern of industry in the valley. Prior to this innovation the key to the success of the textile industry was an abundance of flax and the utilisation of the power in the many fast flowing streams which fed the Six Mile Water, combined with the skill of local people gained previously in the cottage industry.

There was a tremendous variety of water powered mills. Many corn mills existed from earliest times, of course, but water-powered mills for starch, logwood and even snuff were to be found in this locality.

For steam power, however, coal in bulk and a plentiful supply of labour were required and here, Ballyclare town, had a distinct advantage. After 1877, when the narrow gauge railway linked Ballyclare, then later Doagh, to the port at Larne, regular supplies of coal helped to effect a significant expansion in the steam powered industries in the town.

The growth of Ballyclare was due to the success of the linen bleaching and finishing firm, Kirkpatrick Bros, known locally as 'The Green', and the paper mill. Both of these businesses achieved a quality of product which brought acclaim from the rest of Britain. The success of the 'Green' can be judged from the amount of cloth brought from the rest of Ulster, mostly the Lagan Valley, to be finished in Ballyclare. Their expertise had been developed from grass bleaching to a chemical process using huge quantities of water and vitriol. The paper mill had begun in a small way in the 18th century but a move to a site at Milltown on the route to Templepatrick, and the formation of the North of Ireland Paper Mill Company in 1870, brought a more professional management approach to the enterprise and a gradual expansion in paper making took place. By the turn of the century and until the 1940s it was recognised as one of the principal paper mills in the United Kingdom. Ballyclare paper, used for newspapers, books, even Guinness labels, was known throughout Britain and Ireland, and the town was literally 'Paper Town'. In 1951 the mill closed much to the distress of locals who found it hard to accept the inevitability of such a decision, especially as the machinery was speedily sold to a paper mill in Devon. Soon many skilled paper workers followed it there. Its early success had been due to the local abundance of pure water and best quality linen rags. Its weakness as an economic business arose when, with the exception of water, the raw materials - wood celluose and kaolin clay - and coal for steam power, had to be brought from Larne.

From the late 19th century there was a flourishing foundry at Ballyclare but its decline and eventual closure came in the 1950s, a time of fearsome industrial depression in Ballyclare.

Presently the town of Ballyclare has mainly service industries and, owing to its situation just off the busy route between Belfast Airport and Larne, warehousing has become an important activity. It is interesting, though, that recently a firm on the site of the Green, has been experimenting successfully in combining natural flax and synthetic fibres. It is a small echo of the area's illustrious past in the textile trade.

Until two years ago the larger of the paper mill chimneys remained as a landmark in the Six Mile valley but two years ago it succumbed to the demolition skills of Fred Dibnah and almost every trace of the mill complex has now disappeared. Sadly Paper Town exists only in the memory of Ballyclare's older residents.

KIRKPATRICK BROS BLEACH AND DYE WORKS, *c.*1910

One of the oldest bleach works in Ireland was established on this site towards the middle of the 18th century. This main office block was built around the turn of the present century. The Green closed in 1966 but this building and the works are now occupied by a textile business, Kirkpatrick-Linron (Ballyclare) Ltd specialising in combining flax and synthetic fibres. However the decline of this great bleaching firm, watching the scrapping of the machinery and the subsequent deterioration of the entire site has proved a harrowing experience for hundreds of Ballyclare folk whose working lives used to centre on this establishment. (G. McKeown Coll.)

GRASS BLEACHING AT KIRKPATRICK BROS, 1934

This was the last field of handkerchiefs to be grass bleached at the Green. Herbie Watts, Ned Hollis and Johnny Millar are stretching the hanks out to their full length. This traditional method was replaced by the use of vitriol. During the period of peak production, around 1918, three thousand pieces of linen, principally handkerchiefs for export, were processed weekly at the Green. The greatest total output for one week was 110 tons when over 500 people were employed at the works. It scarcely seems surprising that Bob Grange, an employee here at this time, was on hand to make sure that the historic occasion was captured for posterity. (R.T.Grange)

WASH WHEELS IN THE GREEN, *c*.1961
These wheels seen here in Kirkpatrick Bros bleach green shortly before they were demolished in 1962, were one of the earliest methods of washing cloth by machinery. Made entirely of sycamore, each wheel was divided into five compartments, each containing about forty yards of cloth. The water reached the material by way of a hollow steel cylinder on which the wheel revolved. Later wash mills also made of wood, were introduced to speed up production. (T. Black)

31

THE PAPER MILL, MILLTOWN, *c.*1910

The many buildings in the foreground of the mill contain the Salle (pronounced locally 'Saul') where the finished paper was cut, sheeted, counted and prepared for dispatch by ladies with the nimblest fingers in Ballyclare. A horse and wagon cross the bridge over the river beside the canteen, which in effect was simply a room for heating meals brought by the workers in suitable containers. This is the only building in the huge paper mill complex standing today. Behind it are the houses for the management staff in the works. The boiler house is directly between the two chimneys, with the power house sticking up to its left. The lone cow emphasises the rural nature of the mill's surroundings. Today by contrast the site hums with the noise from trucks in a warehousing and transport depot.
(G. McKeown Coll.)

WASTE DEPARTMENT, BALLYCLARE
PAPER MILL, 1939

Waste paper became a vital replacement for increasingly scarce supplies of foreign wood pulp just before, during and after the Second World War. The workers in this department sorted the waste by hand into the different grades – pure white, browns and cardboard. This was an arduous and unpleasant task.

Anticipating a shortage, the paper mill had stored large quantities of waste paper in railway sidings throughout Ulster only to have it requisitioned by the government and shipped to Britain once the war started. (T. Peoples Coll.)

ENGINEERING SHOP, PAPER MILL, *c*.1900

Here all engineering maintenance was undertaken. At this time around twenty-two men, including stokers, were attached to this shop. There were four 'Lancashire' type boilers to be stoked manually and maintained. The engineer, seen typically with 'hard' hat, is Mr J. Montgomery. The unguarded drive belts and other machines in the background were hazards common enough in any industrial works during this period but the paper mill workers also often suffered the loss of fingers in the guillotines and cutting machines. A small sum of money and a job for life was the usual compensation for such occupational mutilation. (Mrs R. Surgeoner Coll.)

MACHINE CREWS, PAPER MILL, *c*.1905

Each of the two large calendar machines seen here had a crew overseeing their operation. There were four such machines in the mill at this time.The view is taken at the dry end of the run with the finished paper reeled. It had begun down the line at the wet end, a mixture of water, pulp and additives being sprayed on to wire gauze and felt rollers and then dried. The men are barefooted because a wet floor, even at the dry end, prevented dust settling on the finished paper. This reeled paper was ready to be cut for dispatch. (J. Cunningham)

RAILWAYS

It is often a surprise to new residents in Ballyclare to discover that two railways used to run into the town. A little observation, though, should quickly indicate that the present tyre service depot at the foot of the Hillhead Road, was until it closed in the 1950s, the terminus of the LMS broad gauge branch line to Belfast. Yet the broad gauge railway somehow never achieved the impact of the other narrow gauge system with Ballyclare folk. The branch of the Ballymena - Larne narrow gauge line had the significant advantage of being there first and, though it could never boast speed or reliability among its assets, it had character and, especially in its early days, a distinct novelty value.

By contrast, it appears that, when the broad gauge line opened in 1884, it had some opposition. Archibald McIlroy described the village before the line to Belfast opened:

The place was neither more nor less than a quiet and secluded country village. Railway trains were only heard from afar, the shriek of the whistle coming to us over miles of quiet country. As children we were awakened from sleep during the night by the sound of this lonely, weird whistle as the engine was engaged in shunting operations at the distant station and we were wont to imagine that it betokened distress.

Railway travelling was not popular with our villagers. We preferred making the journey to and from the city by Johnny Glenn's post-car which covered the distance three times each week, the horse, a veteran of long experience, being turned out to graze on the sides of the road during the off days.

The farmers, when not requiring to take their horses on market days, were accustomed to walk the distance (24 miles) there and back, carrying large baskets of butter and eggs.

The narrow gauge was essentially a freight line. Its viability always depended upon bringing coal to the bleach works using a large store yard at Ballyclare station and, using the special siding into the works carrying coal and other raw materials to the paper mill. Indeed the paper mill and the narrow gauge line were entirely interdependent. Along the route from Larne, the waggons also supplied many heavy goods, especially timber and coal, to the many little wayside stations. From these the farm carts could collect the vital supplies for use at home. In the other direction, livestock and other goods and materials, such as bauxite and iron ore from Ballynure and Ballyboley halts, were taken for shipment at Larne. At one stage even Ballyeaston

had its own halt; situated over a mile away it was not exactly close to the village.

Unlike its broad gauge rival, the narrow gauge railway opened to great acclaim and with a splendid ceremony. The first train to arrive on the opening day, Monday 30th July 1877, was greeted with a great carnival and celebration. The Duke of Marlborough, then Lord Lieutenant of Ireland, arrived in Larne by steamer and proceeded to Ballyclare on the special train. A huge crowd had gathered to cheer the vice regal party at the station and the village brass band played the National Anthem. The train with the party back on board moved to the paper mill works. Having been shown through the various processes, their graces made their way by horse drawn carriage to Shane's Castle at Antrim. Ballyclare was gaily decorated for the occasion and the distinguished visitors were given a stirring reception by the cheering throng. At this period there were some dilapidated cottages at the head of the square and these had been tactfully hidden from their view by large screens covered with the greetings "Welcome to Marlborough" and "God Save the Queen".

In its early days the line was thronged with large crowds enjoying the novelty of rail travel and the spartan freight cars had to be adapted to carry passengers. Until the line closed along with the Paper Mill in 1951, this railway provided a very popular day out for many, indeed the only day out, going by train to Larne and sometimes even, across the channel to the exotic resorts of Islandmagee. Many older folk still recall memories of such outings with pleasure.

Although the effective life of the broad gauge railway was much shorter and, therefore, less significant than the narrow gauge, each line in its own way did make an important, economic contribution to the development of Ballyclare and its hinterland. The railways, too, broadened the view of country people and extended their horizons – even beyond Islandmagee. Ballyclare's isolation was a lot less complete thereafter and life in the village could never return to the serenity described by McIlroy. Such is the march of progress.

BROAD GAUGE RAILWAY STATION, BALLYCLARE, *c.*1912

This view is from the Hillhead Road, looking towards its junction with the Mill Road. The houses in the centre were named Railway Terrace and remain today. The four oil lamps were placed here and arrangements for lighting and maintaining them were made by the Ballyclare Lighting Association, financed by collections from local residents. This railway station eventually became the bus depot, then a car salesroom and garage. Today it is a tyre workshop keeping up the site's transport connections. Indeed the large engine shed is still in use as a store. (G. McKeown Coll.)

BROAD GAUGE STATION, FACING EAST 1936

The row of houses in the background is the Hillhead Road. The stationmaster's house is to be seen directly behind the group of men standing at the station. Beside it is the hut comprising the former headquarters of the East Antrim Harriers. When this branch line to Belfast closed in the late 1940s, this area was used as a bus station and the freight shed beyond the buffers was the bus maintenance garage. The locomotive shed behind the crane is used today by the tyre depot on the site. Indeed the station offices hidden here by the train and freight shed are this firm's offices. A section of the railway platform also survives within this block. (R. T. Grange Coll.)

BROAD GAUGE STATION STAFF AND ENGINE CREW, 1923

It is surprising just how many men were employed here. Indeed working on the railways was a highly prized occupation. The station master in a town, here Mr W. J. Orr in the long coat, had the same status as the schoolmaster and was respected in the community. George McKeown is sixth from the right and Sam Armstrong, Guard, is seen on the extreme right. The windmill was used to pump water for the engines as Ballyclare had no mains supply until the 1950s. (G. McKeown Coll.)

NARROW GAUGE STATION, 1936

This view looks towards the paper mill and Doagh through the Main Street bridge. The station building is on the right and behind it a coal yard with its siding can be seen. The bridge (621) is over the Six Mile Water and part of this parapet still exists though the covering of railway sleepers over the river has gone. Through the bridge towards Doagh were the cattle dock and pens and on the left is the yard gantry for lifting coal containers from rail wagons. Behind the station building on Main Street the apex of the Reo Cinema can be identified. To the right of the general freight siding on the right is the area known as McConnell's yard, where among other activities, cattle were slaughtered for the town's butchers, and horses were stabled, cars garaged and coffins made for a family undertaking business. (R. T. Grange Coll.)

NARROW GAUGE STATION STAFF AND ENGINE CREW, *c.*1920

A coal train at entrance to Ballyclare station, looking east towards Ballynure. The engine with the typical, single, central buffer on the Six Mile Water bridge is No. 109, 'The Bruiser', a regular on this run. The narrow gauge railway was closed for passenger traffic in 1930 and goods in 1933, but it continued to carry pulp and coal to the paper mill until the works closed in 1950.

D. Warwick (driver), W. J. Orr (stationmaster), T. Marshall, S. McCullough (fireman), R. Ireland (guard) J. Stewart (driver). (G. McKeown Coll.)

STEAM LORRY AT NARROW GAUGE STATION, *c.*1920

Coal for the Green was transported the short distance between the station and the works in this steam lorry one of the two, the Sentinel or the Foden, owned at different times by the works. At this time the steamer was a familiar sight chugging up the Green Road Brae with coal, or taking finished cloth to Belfast. Here the coal was clearly shovelled on to the lorry but a few years later the coal was brought from Larne in specially designed rail containers and lifted on to the lorry by crane, pioneering this type of coal containerisation. Eventually the works reverted to shovelling the coal onto McConnell's petrol lorries. This firm held the contract until the nationalisation of road transport in 1937. Two men were needed to drive the lorry, one worked the controls and the other steered. The men are, from left to right - Ned Green, John Woodside, Tom Craig and David McClean. (G. McKeown Coll.)

BALLYCLARE RAILWAY JUNCTION, 1936

This station was close to Mossley where the L.M.S. Belfast to Ballymena line crossed over the Belfast to Larne Road about half a mile from Corr's Corner roadhouse. In the late 1960s this level crossing became unnecessary when the busy trunk road was upgraded and a bridge built over the railway, thus speeding up the flow of road traffic. Now almost all trace of the station has disappeared. It was so named because the line to Ballyclare branched off between here and the Ballyrobert level crossing about two miles beyond. In addition to the buildings seen here there was also a large signal cabin just opposite the stationmaster's house on the right. (J. McKinney Coll.)

EDUCATION

Without doubt the Scots presbyterian background of the people of the Six Mile Valley accounts for their regard for education. Literacy, and in particular, regular reading of the Bible was esteemed highly. Indeed it has been recognised that in the 18th and 19th centuries Ulster, with Scotland enjoyed standards of literacy unsurpassed anywhere in Europe. Nevertheless it still seems surprising to learn that the poet William Percy, born in the 1780s in Ballyeaston could have obtained such an extensive, early education. Later, a teacher in the Ballyclare area, he described how, when he went to school, at the age of five, he had already read through the Bible. He was not an especially privileged child, his father was a weaver with twelve other children, and he did not consider his own achievement remarkable. Significantly in Ballyeaston in the 1790s there was a school already in ruins - forty years before any subsidies from the National Board. Samuel Miskimmin, the distinguished historian who was born in Ballyclare, passed through the village in July 1808 and was saddened to see his old school a desolate ruin:

As I passed through, I looked for the little schoolhouse where I learned to read — it was now a desolate ruin, and seemed to 'ask from my heart the homage of a sigh.'

Another indication of the interest in education in this area is the number of book clubs which flourished and the range and number of volumes they contained. There were only thirty houses in Doagh in the 1770s but the village supported two clubs and there were others in the immediate area. In 1868 there was a very large book club in Ballyclare and members could choose from such titles as Jane Eyre and the works of Sheridan and, of course, Burns.

In 1870 Samuel Corry had a flourishing printing business in Ballyclare and reprinted the poems of the well known weaver poet James Campbell from Ballynure. Indeed the network of weaver poets in Ulster in the late 18th and early 19th centuries included many from the Six Mile Valley, notably Samuel Thompson from Templepatrick and Thomas Beggs of Ballyclare. Their popularity in this district indicates a taste for good verse.

In 1831 a system of national schools was introduced. Centralised in Dublin, grants were awarded to suitable applicants presenting cases for deserving schools, towards the cost of teaching requisites, buildings and teachers' salaries. Around this period there was a proliferation of local schools funded jointly by public subscription and the National Board. By the end of the 19th century, within a five mile radius of Ballyclare, upwards of thirty such national schools were in operation. However conditions were often primitive and in 1856 an inspector described one of the two Ballyclare national schools:

There is standing room for 32 only, breathing space for 24 only and yet there were 75 present on the day of my visit with no means to ventilate the room properly. I look upon it as inhuman to permit so many children to congregate together in so small and wretched a cabin and the teacher would be more than human who could effect a particle of good in it.

In 1881 a grand new two storied building was opened in Ballyclare just off the main square. This was to serve pupils, in separate boys and girls schools, from an amalgamation of two out-dated buildings, one fondly known as 'the Wooden Box' and another nicknamed 'Fractions' School' a natural consequence of the master's prowess in arithmetic. The conditions in this latter establishment were marginally worse than the rival school in Tow Loanin'. Overcrowding, however, has always been a feature of Ballyclare schools, an inevitable result of regular periods of population expansion.

With close to 3000 children at school in the town today Ballyclare can claim to be as important a centre for education as its markets have always been in the past for other young livestock.

BALLYCLARE INTERMEDIATE SCHOOL, NORTH END, *c.*1928

A school begun by Miss Catherine Aiken in Doagh in 1902, moved to premises in Ballyclare Square soon afterwards. In 1918 it was amalgamated with another school and then as Ballyclare Intermediate School, prepared pupils for intermediate and commercial examinations. After a spell above a butcher's shop at North End it moved further up the Rashee Road where it became Ballyclare High School. The group above, includes the Ainsley twins in the front row and the Rowland brothers, Tim to the far right of the front row and Robin, later Judge Rowland, second from the right in the row behind his brother. (L. Gordon Coll.)

NATIONAL SCHOOL, BALLYCLARE. JULY 1904

BOYS' NATIONAL SCHOOL, BALLYCLARE, 1904

Master William McKean on the right, and the monitor William James Boyd on the left of this row, are seen with the entire Boys' School. The monitor was simply a young person preparing for acceptance as a teacher, who supervised the younger children. There were as many girls then attending a separate school in the same building. The Eton collars were not unusual at this time but it must be noted that it was known in advance that a photograph was to be taken and most parents dressed children for the occasion. Those appearing shabby or without shoes were usually hidden in the background. When he was 89 Robert Grange, armed with a magnifying glass and the school register was able to identify 101 out of the 119 boys seen here. He himself is twelfth from the left in the third row from the front. Mr McKean came each day by pony and trap from Straid and it was often Robert Grange's job to go to McConnell's yard and feed the pony. (J. Cunningham)

STAFF OF BALLYCLARE BOYS' AND GIRLS' NATIONAL SCHOOLS, 1904

Such photographs of national school staffs are, surprisingly, quite rare. This was obviously taken on the same day as the groups of girls and boys, and the staff invited some friends to be included. We can be sure there were no bare feet in this group. We know from the accounts of his scholars that Mr McKean was indeed as stern as his expression suggests. (Back Row,left to right) Miss N. Waide (Girls' School Principal),

Mr J. Reid (visitor), Mr J. Hadden, Mr J. C. Stewart, visitor. (Front Row,left to right) Miss M. Reid, Mr W. McKean (Boys' School Principal), Miss M. Smyth.

Mr James Hadden later married Miss Norah Waide and succeeded his uncle, William McKean, as Principal of the Boys School in 1912. (J. Cunningham)

FRACTIONS' SCHOOL

In 1845, David John McCune came as master to Ballyclare No. 2 National School. He was an eccentric, clever teacher and he was one of the few to attain the Board's classification of grade 1, First Class Division. His speciality was arithmetic and an ability to perform "wonderful geometrical and algebraical feats" earned him the nickname 'Fractions'. Even today, locals refer to the site of his building as 'Fractions' School'. For information on this character we are lucky to have had Archibald McIlroy the local author as a pupil at his school. Historian, Robert Grange, also recorded much about Fractions that he heard from his mother, a pupil at the Girls' School just above Mr McCune's academy for boys.

Their descriptions say much about the man and the school.

The master. . . was a tall, well-built, fresh complexioned man with a somewhat marked cast of features, keen, grey eyes, prominent nose and a firmly set mouth. (McIlroy)

The windows had small panes of glass and when school finished for the day these were covered with wooden shutters which hung downwards on chains during the day. Sanitary arrangements were entirely absent, when nature called the pupils simply adjourned to the nearby fields. Occasionally when an entire class was permitted to leave they had no inclination for a speedy return so a second party was organised to bring the wanderers back to the seat of learning and often they in turn got lost. He lived in one of the small thatched cottages which nestled at the foot of Murphy's Hill in a small townland known as Cowterstoon. He owned a donkey and small cart and they - McCune and his small, delicate daughter - would be seen daily making the trip down the Green Road together, David John in his black frock coat and stove-pipe hat and she comfortably tucked up in the wee cart. (R. Grange)

Fractions apparently used the local dialect liberally and had a habit of boasting of his past achievements:

'Jest think boys ', he would say, 'O Tam Forsythe, noo a professor in Cambridge University, writing tae me regularly an' tellin' me he attributes a' his success tae the guid grindin' he got frae me, an' tae my discernment in finnin' oot what was in 'im. (McIlroy)

He was, surprisingly, keen on elocution and he gave this advice to his pupils:

"Hold up yer heids like men an' dinnae be fear'd tae let oot yer voices." (McIroy)

Parents though, preferred the essentials and one farmer told the Master:

"Keep him at readin', writin', an' coontin', dinna waste his time on jography; for efter a' whor's the use o' his learnin' the names o' a wheen o' places he's nivver likely tae see." (McIlroy)

Yet he was kind, even if his treats were unorthodox:

In the cold frosty days of Winter he always kept a large metal pot filled to the brim with delicious soup, made by himself, simmering on the peat fire and at regular intervals during the day a generous helping was ladled into the bowls which he himself provided for each child." (R. Grange)

Sometimes he sent out for delicacies. 'Black Lumps' were large balls of dark sticky toffee.

"Half an hour before closing time the longed for and ever-welcome black lumps would be brought forth from the hidden resources of the master's coat-tail pockets, and handed round the class. The process began with the head boy, who was allowed to suck the lump for all too short a period, when he would be required to relinquish it to his next neighbour, Fractions watching the while that no boy detained the luxury too long, or sank his teeth in it." (McIlroy)

Sadly Fractions' decline began with a personal tragedy. His delicate daughter died and with her seemed to die the vigour so effectively portrayed by McIlroy. An inspector's report in 1875 reprimanded him for "low proficiency in Arithmetic" of all things! He retired in June 1880 but the talent and exploits of Fractions were not forgotten in Ballyclare.

'FRACTIONS' SCHOOL, MARKET SQUARE,
BALLYCLARE. 1906

Although it ceased to be a national school building in 1881 the old school was used to accommodate the Urban Council for public meetings and even served as a dental surgery for some time before its demolition in the 1930s. Evidently it also saw good service as a public noticeboard. Fortunately the national school plaque, clearly seen in the photograph, was preserved and today is set into a garden of a house on the Rashee Road. The steps at the side formerly gave access to the girls school, the boys being accommodated on the ground floor. It was in this academy that David John McCune, 'Fractions', would boast to his ill clad band of scholars "Noo boys a hae been a roun' the world - an' a wheen o' ither places forbye" (J. Cunningham)

OCCASIONS AND ENTERTAINMENT

No event could ever compete with the annual extravaganza of the May Fair but there were many other opportunities for amusement in Ballyclare. In particular, coronations and royal jubilees stirred up ardent patriotic fervour in the town. These took the usual form of decorating the streets with flags and bunting, lighting bonfires on the Craig Hill and holding fancy dress parades. And, of course, each year the 12th of July brought its usual pageantry to the streets.

There have been, over the years few occasions when the mood on the streets was gloomy or even ugly, but the paper mill strike in 1911 did work up passion in the workers. And in 1914 when the group of First World War volunteers made their way down the street to the station, those who lined the route understandably had a feeling of pride mixed with apprehension. At the end of last century a very different procession went up Main Street. A child's body had been found in the river; no parent could be found and the local women dressed the body in white and carried the pathetic little bundle to the paupers' cemetery at Ballycorr.

Dancing was always popular in the district and before the town hall became the Mecca for dancers in East Antrim, a colourful establishment existed in Caddy's Row beside the bridge. Rejoicing under the title of "The Greasy Pig" its reputation was not entirely respectable and it was ironic that the premises eventually became the Ballyclare headquarters of the Salvation Army. Before its renovation in 1935, conditions in the town hall for dancing were rather primitive. The ladies' dressing room was created by the use of screens down in the Market House where normally dead pigs were weighed, and tea for the refreshments was brewed outside in the square. At this time no public conveniences existed in the town but those requesting such facilities at dances were quietly advised of the proximity of the many wide open spaces out towards Doagh.

The town hall was the venue for plays, concerts and socials. The town eventually had a cinema but most Ballyclare folk saw their first films in a famous picture house out at Cogry Mill. This was so popular that certain performances had to be reserved for mill workers, with outsiders restricted to other shows. Variety concerts in the town hall were popular and in the early days of the Reo Cinema there were always 'artistes' performing, with the films as part of an evening's entertainment. In the country halls around Ballyclare much of the best entertainment was derived from heckling the often indifferent performers who were brave enough to face these fickle audiences. Church socials were also popular but often equally unruly.

The Summer season brought picnics and the site of one of these could always be detected from the stack of bicycles propped up against the field hedges. Sunday nights were for walks around the roads and often there would be a regular convoy from Ballyclare to Ballylinney, Ballyeaston, Straid or Ballynure. Fishing along the banks of the Six Mile was pleasant then too and swimming was possible in the river especially in well-known deep holes or 'carries' out towards Whitepark.

But for many, the best pastime was simply a crack at the 'Brig', the traditional centre for the exchange of daily gossip and banter. Leaning over the Six Mile bridge on a summer evening was very relaxing especially with no traffic roar to blunt your neighbour's conversation. In such serenity did folk in Ballyclare patiently await the May Fair - or discuss its aftermath.

ROYAL OCCASION, 1902

The photograph is dated 1906 but can surely only be of the coronation of Edward V11 four years earlier. His picture and his consort's clearly appear on the decorations of this and another photograph certainly taken at the same time. The row of houses is Railway Terrace with the broad gauge railway station behind the trees. At the end of this row was the junction of the Mill road and the Hillhead road both leading to Belfast. By a long tradition, royal occasions brought great festivity to Ballyclare.

At Queen Victoria's Jubilee in 1897 a bonfire built in the Square was so large that it cracked windows of properties nearby. Sometimes the Six Mile river was alight with fire on rafts in the water. Typically, last century Chinese style lanterns covered the branches of a large tree in Ollar Lodge in Lower Main Street and premises on the streets and square were always gaily decorated. (J. Cunningham)

PAPER MILL STRIKE, 1911

The first stirrings of the fervour of trade unionism appeared in Ballyclare in 1910 and soon afterwards a bitter strike began in the Green. When it was eventually settled and unrest spread to the paper mill many women workers refused to join the strike and had to be escorted to the works by about 100 constables brought in to deal with the unrest from outside the town. Here they are seen making their way up Main Street returning from work under the protection of the police. The Thatch Inn is on the right. (J. Cunningham; Mr S. Graham Coll.)

OFF TO THE FIRST WORLD WAR,
18th SEPTEMBER 1914

On 16th September 1914 recruitment for the Ulster Division opened in the town hall, Ballyclare and over 100 men joined up on the first day. Two days later at noon these men formed up and led by the village brass band, the column marched to the broad gauge railway station. All the works had been closed for the day and the crowds gathered here and sang with the band 'Will ye no come back again?' Amidst wild cheering and the sound of detonators exploding on the rails, the first contingent of volunteers left for training at Clandeboye Camp. Very few were ever to return. (J. Cunningham)

WEDDING ON MAIN STREET, *c.*1911

The bride and groom emerge from the Non-Subscribing Presbyterian Church on Main Street. A church was established on this site in 1646, the oldest congregation in Ballyclare. The drapery shop on the right is The Blue House owned by the Cunningham family to which the photographer belonged. They lived in the house next to the shop. Some time later it was incorporated into the shop premises. The horse and carriage is probably that of Samuel Milliken who undertook weddings and funerals in Ballyclare at this time. He was succeeded by the McConnell family who carried on a very successful transport and undertaking business up until quite recently. (J.Cunningham)

A COUNTRY WEDDING, 20th JULY 1925

The happy couple are Andy Clements from Headwood, a district between Ballynure and Larne, and Mary Sloan from Straid and the photograph has been taken outside the bride's house, The Dairy, close to Straid. In the doorway on the left is James Sloan the bride's father and master of Straid school for many years. His other daughters, Belle who taught with him in Straid, Jean, Lottie and Marjory are there too and bear a distinct family resemblance. James, his son is on the left of the front row. Mr Alex Woodside, master of Tildarg school is sitting at the end of the front row. The sister of the bridegroom, Mary Clements, became his wife.

The balding Rev. Andrew Scott from Ballynure church can be seen at the back. (G. McKeown)

55

KIRKPATRICK BROS STAFF OUTING, *c.*1920

A day spent on cast iron garden seats on the back of this old Maudsley lorry with its solid tyres could not have been a very pleasant experience. It seems from Delargy's garage in the background that their destination was probably Cushendall.

The driver, David Crawford is in the middle of the group in front, with Tommy Currie on his right. Sammy Hunter is on the right at the back of the lorry. (L. Gordon Coll.)

CORONATION CELEBRATIONS AT THE GREEN, 1937

The folding loft of the Kirkpatrick Bros works is decorated for the Coronation of King George VI. Crowned in the centre is Lily Beggs, the Organdie Queen. The firm was justly proud of their specialist skills in finishing this beautiful but difficult material. In the late 1940s a special bolt of the cloth, dyed and finished at the works, was sent by request to the royal household. Major H. B. McCance (Managing Director) can be seen with spectacles on the far right, with his wife nearby in the fox fur. (L. Gordon Coll.)

57

BALLYCLARE MINSTREL TROUPE, early 1900s

Also known as 'McFarlane's String Band' this group dressed for stage performances in a collection of multi-coloured costumes like pierrots at seaside shows. They 'blacked up' using burnt cork with their large moustaches gummed back to their faces. Bob McFarlane, the leader,(third from left, front row) an extremely witty man, was also an expert flautist. Frank Blair, the popular local comedian is second from the right in the front row. Bob McFarlane's band once accompanied the town's traders on an August Bank Holiday outing to Portrush by train. This was popularly known in Ballyclare as The Robbers' Excursion. (G. McKeown Coll.)

58

BALLYCLARE VICTORIA FLUTE BAND, 1932

In the early years of this century, the village flute band under the direction of Bob McFarlane was quite small and played at local functions such as picnics, political meetings and orange processions. After the First World War this band was formed in 1918 through the untiring efforts of Bob McFarlane and he included Victoria in its name. The band was also dominated by McFarlanes, for at one time Bob and four of his sons marched side by side in the Victoria. For a long time peaked caps comprised their only uniform. This cup is the Junior Section, Grade II Championship of the N.I. Bands Association. Since 1960 the band has won the Association's Senior World Championship eighteen times, including a record ten times in succession between 1975 and 1984. (G. McKeown)

PUBS, POEMS AND PASTIMES

It is common knowledge that Ballyclare has always been famous for the number of pubs it can support, but it is not so widely known why this has been so. Many farmers from the area between Ballyclare and Ballymena, making their way to market in Belfast in the past, with a cartload of produce, would break their journey in Ballyclare. Arriving in the evening they would put up at an inn, stable the horses, and rest until around three o'clock in the morning when the villagers in their beds would hear the sound of the cart wheels creaking towards Belfast. Thus there was good business for such inns. At the same time it must be acknowledged that Ballyclare has never been renowned for temperance and its many pubs have always had a strong trade. The attitude to alcohol is nicely summed up by one ardent drinker's creed: *"I'm a teetotaller, but no' a bigoted yin."* At one time, at the foot of the town, there were three public houses side by side, while further up Main Street a Temperance Hotel and a pub operated quite happily side by side.

It is interesting to look at the character of the various pubs, hotels and inns. In most cases they had some distinctive feature, either a tradition, a pastime or a sport, associated with the establishment, often connected with the interests of the publican. 'Shines' Service got his name from his commendable habit, not always strictly observed elsewhere, of diligently and endlessly polishing the glasses.

R. T. Wilson Baird's establishment (not to be confused with his brother Francis Baird's, two doors down, in lower Main Street) was known as The Ollardale Hotel and sported a very unusual collection of antiquities and curios. A contemporary guide book states that this attraction brought many tourists into the town. Ballyclare could be a convenient stop for cross-channel visitors travelling in horse-drawn brakes to the port at Larne. There was 'Corny Crymble's Stone', weighing nearly a ton and of doubtful origin, a holy water stoup found in a local chimney, a quern, an old pike, two artillery pieces and some spinning wheels. Sadly most of these have since disappeared. Incredibly, in a small garden attached to the Ollardale Hotel, was a network of underground passages, a fernery, fountain, fishpond and croquet and badminton courts, camera obscura, an apiary and an aviary. Robert was also a well known practical joker and tourists in his caves were often startled to hear a cast iron lion roar, a hidden local having been placed here for the

stunt before the tour commenced. He had invented a game called "Bal-clare", played on a small court by four persons using small cricket bats and a soccer ball hanging from a wire line. The Ollardale Hotel actually stood on the site of the small thatched cottage where Samuel McSkimmin, the historian of Carrickfergus, had been born.

Then there was Robert Baird's Band, a motley crew who paraded the streets on important occasions dressed in a variety of multi-coloured garments and playing the drums, penny tin whistles, bugles, horns, corncrakes and flutes. Robert Baird also regularly organised firework displays during such celebrations. Whatever the consumption of alcohol in Ballyclare at other times of the year there is no doubt that with so many visitors in town, it reached prodigious proportions during the annual May Fair. The most telling comment on this comes in a report in the *Larne Weekly Telegraph* of 29th May 1929, in connection with the opening of the Ballymullock reservoir in Larne:

On Tuesday the formal turning-on of the water into the new reservoir took place. Ballyclare May Fair took place on the same day. There is no necessary connection between the two things. Water is not the principal beverage consumed in Ballyclare on the big day.

Whatever the weather, Ballyclare has never been a dry town - certainly not during its famous fair days.

FRANCIS BAIRD'S PUBLIC HOUSE, *c.*1908

This public house at the corner of Main Street and Mill Road was joined on to Wilson's Row, a terrace of houses, and some of its residents are, no doubt, included in this group. Affluence is certainly not in evidence here. In more recent times this became John Baird's public house but the building with its distinctive, ornate plaster work was sadly demolished in the 1960s to give better access to vehicles, especially buses, into Main Street. Among those who mourned its fate were many who missed its function more than its appearance. This was a popular inn as it had separate entrances in Main Street and Wilson's Row allowing patrons to nip in or out while keeping their visit a secret from any prying eyes. (J. Cunningham)

EAST ANTRIM HARRIERS IN THE OLLARDALE GARDEN, 1908

The harriers were formed in 1907 and this early photograph was taken behind the Ollardale Hotel in lower Main Street. R. T. Wilson Baird, the owner, gave the club support. His brother, Frank, a neighbouring publican, (back row, far right) was a very active sportsman. He had been a notable athlete in his youth and he also enjoyed horse and greyhound racing and coursing. (J. Cunningham)

OLLARDALE FOOTBALL TEAM, OLLARDALE
GARDEN, 1907

This club, formed in 1904 in Ballyclare as Avondale, later changed its name to Ollardale when R. T. Wilson Baird (first left, back row) the owner of the Ollardale Hotel in lower Main Street provided accommodation for meetings and a dressing room. John Baird (third right, front row) nephew of the hotel's owner and son of Frank Baird, was one of the team's earliest players. With its great rival, Green Rangers, the team dominated the pre-First World War football scene in Ballyclare. Hugh McCrone (Chairman) is first right in the front row. He provided the team's pitch at his Doagh Road farm. The thatched shelter, a stone lion and a minature house, part of the Ollardale garden's curios are seen in the background. (J. Cunningham)

THE THATCH INN, MAIN STREET, BALLYCLARE,
c.1920
This inn, owned by Houston Craig, was demolished in 1926 to
make way for a branch of the Ulster Bank. Frank Blair's lament
showed his obvious disgust at such a tragedy.

And now at last wae grief and pain, I see The Thatch
it has been slain,
That dear auld hoose o' memory sweet, has disappeared clean
off oor street.
To me it seems a desecration, a loss to us and all the nation,
But in its place, no doubt, will rise, a building of gigantic size
A house of strength, a house of rank – another blinking
Ulster Bank.

(R. T. Grange Coll.)

THE FIVE CORNERS, *c*.1911
This pub still remains one and a half miles north of Ballyclare at the junction of five roads into the town. In the 1930s and early 1940s, Jock Gilmour sat at its fireside reciting verses he had composed about the countryside not far away, where he lived.

(G. McKeown Coll.)

At the Corners Five, man alive, the devil did appear,
He passed us by like wind and sky, and filled our hearts with fear.
Some said he had a pair of horns, others said he had a tail,
For they saw it birling round his head, like the souple of a flail.

THE NORTHERN BAR

Mr Willy Hugh Grange outside his pub, The Northern Bar, at the north-east corner of the Square about 1908. Today the pub, although no longer owned by the Grange family, is appropiately called 'The Grange'. (R. Nelson Coll.)

THE BALLOON INCIDENT

When Jack Grange, the publican of The Northern Bar, Ballyclare, his mother, sister Ruby and two dogs set out for a drive in their little Morris car one Sunday afternoon in November 1941, they couldn't possibly have imagined where they would end up that day. On the way home they had collected a crate of whisky and one of rum from their other bar in Larne. These were in short supply during wartime. Entering Ballyclare along the Ballynure Road Jack saw a strange sight - a barrage balloon drifting overhead. He did not pay much attention at the time but some time afterwards he noticed a cable coming along the middle of the road and it suddenly struck him that it belonged to the balloon which had somehow broken loose from its moorings. When it was about ten yards away Jack knew that he would have to act quickly. He jammed on the brakes, opened the door and pushed his sister out on to the roadway. He then quickly turned round and helped his mother out of the back seat before jumping out himself. Fortunately the dogs had also managed to escape.

The cable caught on to the car, dragging it along for about eighty yards before it sailed into the air as if it had wings, until the car struck a tree and became lodged in the branches. The cable had fouled electricity wires and this subsequently caused a power cut throughout east Antrim. Ruby Grange vividly remembers one part of the escapade. As they were recovering from shock and surprise, a chap got out of a car which had been travelling close behind them and informed them excitedly that he had been following the barrage balloon from Antrim, trying to catch it. She did not need to add that they had just managed this very successfully. The balloon was secured by ropes until more effective help arrived.

Eventually, army and R.A.F. personnel came and released the balloon which drifted off towards the open fields at Skilganaban, followed by the usual curious hordes. When it was brought down by rifle fire, the remains were seized upon and cut into pieces as souvenirs, much to the disapproval of the police and military guards supervising the operation.

The car was also eventually lowered to the ground practically undamaged only to be unaccountably, impounded by the authorities. Perhaps they had got a whiff of what the boot contained. Indeed administrative difficulties took so long that Jack Grange eventually went to the barracks surreptitiously and drove the car home, keeping an eye open to ensure that the sky, as well as the coast, was clear. It is hardly surprising to learn that in the next few weeks record business was done in the Northern Bar where the publican was kept busy recounting his strange experience. At least one scrap of the balloon survives today in a local home, a souvenir of an incident which surely could only happen in Ballyclare!

At Ballyclare Boys National School in 1905 (R. T. Grange Coll.)

ROBERT GRANGE.

It is thanks to Robert Grange that we know so much about people and events of the past in the Six Mile valley. Up to his death in 1990 he was widely acknowledged as Ballyclare's historian and the research he did and the careful records he kept all his life have been invaluable to others interested in the history of the district. His writing is enlivened because, he included details of the characters he knew so well and anecdotes he heard and enjoyed.

He was born in 1896 and went to Ballyclare Boys' National School when he was just three years old. Typically he remembers his first day, trotting along beside an older brother and feeling apprehensive.

When war broke out in 1914 he took 'The King's Shilling' adding on one year to his age to make him eligible for enlistment. He was with the 36th Ulster Division at the Somme and was later wounded in action but recovered to finish the war as an expert signaller with the Royal Engineers. His accounts of this war service are among his finest and most detailed writing. Back in Ballyclare he returned to the works of Kirkpatrick Brothers, as a bleacher and his skill in this work made him indispensible to this firm, then one of the foremost linen finishing works in Ulster. He stayed here until his retirement and it saddened him to see the eventual decline of this local enterprise.

Always one who eagerly joined the 'auld residenters' enjoying a crack at the brig, he also picked up many facts from his mother who, like himself, lived to a ripe old age. Around the

1940s he began to compile a history of the town and district. Eventually he had two large ledgers written in a beautiful, copperplate hand and illustrated with photographs of people and events mentioned in his text.

His description of characters such as the Ballyclare Town Crier were sufficiently vivid to require little illustration.

Dressed in a light blue frock coat and his head adorned with a stove-pipe hat he would sally forth with the Market House hand bell, proclaiming to the residents all important and unusual news. Official and Government proclamations, public meetings, auctions, concerts and such like were all made known to the public in this fashion. One of the earliest of the town ciers was, in the usual Ballyclare manner, nick-named 'The Hangman'. He lived in the Back Street and was a cattle drover. Sammy McClean was the last of the criers in the early years of the present century but he wore no uniform or unusual dress. One of the town's characters used to keep abreast of Sammy on the footpath, the crier always occupied the centre of the street, and at intervals would call out in a loud voice "Ring the bell, Sambo, and ring it again". Sammy would simply halt and give his persecutor a withering glare. After the early 1900s Sammy's cry was heard no more for more modern methods of advertising had arrived to replace voice and bell.

Thanks to Bob Grange, Sammy McClean and many other popular characters have not been forgotten in Ballyclare.

In the Royal Engineers around 1916 (R. T. Grange Coll.)

69

ARCHIBALD MCILROY

Archibald McIlroy was born in 1859 on the Fluther Loanin' in the townland of Ballylinney on the outskirts of Ballyclare. His people were farmers but Artie made his career in the bank. He travelled extensively in Europe, was a member of the county council and had ambitions to enter parliament before ill health intervened. However it was his life as an author which brought him fame especially in Ballyclare, though his books sold well in Britain and even in America. He inherited a natural, droll humour from his grandfather. He tells how this old man was famous for telling amusing ancedotes and singing comic songs which he accompanied on the fiddle. McIlroy himself gave public lectures. One of the most popular was *'Life and Love in an Ulster Village '*, illustrated with a large number of views, many of them, in his words, *'of a very quaint description' and* interspersed with many characteristic anecdotes and droll sayings culled from many quarters, and its popularity was unbounded. Though he didn't admit it there is little doubt that it was modelled on Ballyclare.

He attended three schools in the village and each is described vividly in his books. He had the knack of choosing the most distinctive events and characters and giving them the full treatment. However he was tactful enough to disguise the real people and places by using pseudonyms - Ballyclare became Craig Linnie while the mountainous country north of the village was Tildree, a clever combination of Tildarg and Tardree. Most people, naturally, had a pretty good idea of the true identities. Some of the characters he describes are fascinating:

The "Cadger" was a notable personality in his day - probably a protege of some member of the Tumulty family, for he was a famous prize-fighter, and the strongest man the village had ever seen. His time could not have all been taken up with drinking and boxing, seeing that he built the "Cadger's Close" a number of houses branching off from the main street of the village.

When in his cups, "the Cadger" was a terrible sight, as he paraded the street up and down, stripped to the waist, and challenging any four men to come out and fight with him twelve rounds. People barred their doors and windows, the street being quite deserted when "the Cadger" was known to be in one of his moods. He was wont to boast that he feared neither God nor man. His chest was covered with hair, equal to what grew on another man's head and his arms displayed bunches of muscle to a marvellous extent. (**From When lint was in the bell**).

He often used in his text snatches of the distinctive local dialect and this has given a colourful, authentic picture of every aspect of life in Ballyclare at the end of last century. He was lost on the Lusitania in 1915 when on route to America and sadly, his books nowadays are not well known in his native town.

Archibald McIlroy *c.*1900 (R. T. Grange Coll.)
The McIlroy Store *c.*1920 (R. T. Grange Coll.)

GEORGE McDOWELL, *c.*1910

Geordie McDowell was an old eccentric preacher, very poor and practically illiterate, who was to be found every Saturday night, wet or fine, outside the Blue House on Main Street, warning sinners about the fate which awaited them. If they did not repent, he had the habit of saying, they would waken up dead in the morning standing upright in their coffins. The Cunningham family, living in The Blue House, were very kind to the old man, often giving him food and clothing. John Cunningham also had a shrewd eye for a good subject for his camera and many such Ballyclare characters appeared in front of his lens, often in situations which were obviously heavily staged to look well in a photograph. (J. Cunningham)

TOMMY MARSHALL
Tommy Marshall lived on the Mill Lane, Ballyclare and he controlled the level crossing where the narrow gauge railway siding entered the paper mill. He obviously had a way with goats and it is well known that this large billy was popular and useful with local herds. From the gleam in their eyes it is difficult to detect who stands prouder before the camera, the owner or the magnificent beast. (J. Cunningham)

THE CUNNINGHAM DOGS, *c*.1920

John Cunningham loved dogs and he tried to include one or two in most of his prints. Here they have the central role. These are remarkable photographs considering the exposure time of his camera and they form part of a series of these same dogs in different poses. Here are the dogs at their breakfast of soda farls and boiled eggs and in a tableau which must have tried his skill and patience to set up for the camera. The little terrier appears in the background of many of his photographs. The photographer and his dogs always appear to be enjoying themselves. (J. Cunningham)

FRANK BLAIR, COMEDIAN, *c.*1908

Frank Blair, a talented Ballyclare entertainer moulded himself
on Harry Lauder, the Scots comedian and often dressed on
stage in kilt and sporran. He also, as above,appeared as a
housewife with appropriate patter in his strong Ballyclare
dialect. During the First World War he joined the divisional
concert party,'The Merry Mauves' and was a distinct success.
He tried the professional stage after the war but soon tired of
the constant travelling. He returned to Ballyclare to manage the
local cinema. He emigrated to America eventually and a
farewell concert was held in his honour in the cinema on 28th
November 1930 when he gave his usual recitations including
'The Thatch' and 'Poor Merriet Men' and told his popular yarns.
(J. Cunningham)

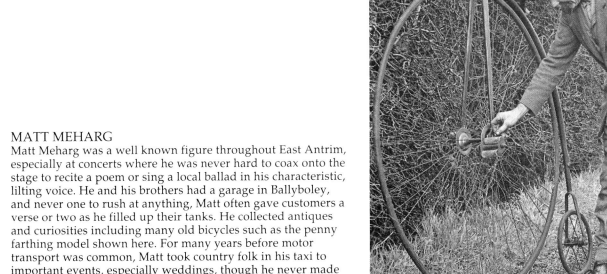

MATT MEHARG
Matt Meharg was a well known figure throughout East Antrim, especially at concerts where he was never hard to coax onto the stage to recite a poem or sing a local ballad in his characteristic, lilting voice. He and his brothers had a garage in Ballyboley, and never one to rush at anything, Matt often gave customers a verse or two as he filled up their tanks. He collected antiques and curiosities including many old bicycles such as the penny farthing model shown here. For many years before motor transport was common, Matt took country folk in his taxi to important events, especially weddings, though he never made the trip to church as a groom himself. He also had a regular run taking a full load of dancers from Ballyclare to the popular ballroom at the Rinkha, Islandmagee. One of Matt's passengers, a groom from Ballyboley, composed a few verses about his chauffeur on his big day: (Miss Eileen Meharg Coll.)

Ballyboley is a spot that is known near and far,
There's a boy up in that country who drives a wedding car.
He's jolly and light- hearted, I hear the people say
And when he takes you for a run he isn't hard to pay.

He is a skilful driver and never does things rash,
He's been driving cars for many years and never had a crash.
So I shall give his name to you, to spell it isn't hard,
His address is Ballyboley and his name is Matt Meharg.

DOAGH AND COGRY

Doagh has had long associations with human settlement and the ruins of St Mary's church, first referred to in 1251, can be seen in Church Lane graveyard. On his ramble from Carrickfergus to Antrim in 1808 Samuel Miskimmin came through Ballyclare to Doagh:

Leaving this place we entered Doagh; this is a small village consisting of about thirty dwelling houses situated on the road leading from Belfast to Ballymena and about ten miles from each place. It contains nothing remarkable except its book clubs which are the most ancient and extensive in this part of the country, the people generally having a taste for literature. Their clubhouse is furnished with a globe, maps etc. Much praise is due to Mr W. Galt for his exertions in promoting these and similar societies instead of the royal sport of cock-fighting so very destructive of the morals of the lower orders of the people.

Doagh grew up around Fisherwick, an elegant hunting lodge of the Marquis of Donegall. It contained, in Miskimmin's time many young trees, shrubberies, walks and fish ponds on which were a pleasure boat and some beautiful swans. There were also stables and kennels and the local inn was the headquarters of the hunting fraternity.

In the late 18th and early 19th centuries the Donegalls gave the area around Doagh a splendour and grandeur certainly not seen elsewhere around Ballyclare. The village was situated at the centre of a great park formed by Sir Arthur Chichester which covered an area of about six square miles and extended from Parkgate to the Thorn Ditch boundary half way between Ballyclare and Doagh.

Doagh has indeed a surprising number of other claims to distinction. William Galt, who was responsible for the establishment of the book club in 1768, also began a sunday school here in 1770, teaching the elements of reading and writing, and this is reputed to be one of the earliest such schools in the country.

Then there was its famous foundry established by Mr John Rowan on the site later incorporated within the premises of Doagh spinning mill just outside the village. Iron implements of a very high quality were made here and gates for fields and the ornate entrances of many large residences in the area. Fisherwick had such a set, and these wrought iron specimens were of the finest craftsmanship. Some remain in place to the present day. The first threshing mill in the country was made in

Doagh foundry and Rowan designed and built a steam powered road vehicle. On 1st January 1836, surrounded on all sides by excited cheering crowds, he drove this to Belfast and it attracted a great deal of attention. This was widely reported in the Belfast newspapers.

Until the recent decline in the textile industry the Doagh Flax Spinning Company was a large concern employing many local people and eventually taking over premises in Belfast. This mill only closed quite recently. Like many other linen centres hockey was, indeed still is, a popular sport in the village and Parkview, the Doagh club's name, has a long record of success in the game.

About two miles from Doagh on the river which fed the mills, was Cogry village. This mainly consisted of a square of the usual mill terrace houses right beside the large Cogry spinning factory. The area around the Cogry mill with its community and scutch and beetling mills, houses and school was completely dominated by the mill owners. One row of houses and a school not so connected were known as Independent Row and Independent School. The main mill was begun in 1845 as a linen business, after a fire had destroyed a corn mill on the site. It was a significant concern for about a century, very innovative and progressive for its time. A cold spinning process was successfully pioneered and a generator using the power of the passing stream provided electricity to make Cogry mill the second mill in Ireland to be so illuminated. Conditions in the mill were, however, less than perfect, especially for the children. These "half timers" began work in the mill at six o'clock in the morning for three hours work, went to school for a spell and then returned to work until six o'clock in the evening.

Cogry Square was demolished in the 1960s the mill having closed in the late 1950s, but today the site has been redeveloped with attractive, modern houses. The substantial old mill buildings are in operation as a very successful engineering business. Even the building which was used as this famous Cogry mill cinema has been preserved - empty except for the flickering ghosts of Charlie Chaplin and other silent movie stars.

NARROW GAUGE RAILWAY STATION, DOAGH, 1930
An extension of the Larne to Ballyclare narrow gauge branch line to Doagh was opened for goods and passenger traffic in 1884. It closed in 1933 with the distinction of having been the last station on this line to open and the first to close. Engine No. 109 (The Bruiser) is seen at the station building which remains today though derelict. Doagh also claimed a station three miles away at Ballypallady on the Belfast to Ballymena L.M.S. line. A horse and trap service took passengers to the upper station. (R. T. Grange Coll.)

DOAGH, *c.*1908

This view looks north, with the road to Ballyclare on the right beside the pump, the route to Antrim on the left and the Ballymena road at the top left. Beside the Rowan Memorial is McConnell's, a Wine and Spirit Merchant. In the 18th century this was famous as Farrell's Inn and accommodated the overflow of the Marquis of Donegall's guests from his hunting lodge at Fisherwick, his fine house just outside the village. At the top of the village on the left beside the telegraph pole is the school, while beyond smoke may just be seen coming from the chimney of the spinning mill. This was the site of Rowan's foundry. (G. McKeown Coll.)

DOAGH VILLAGE, Late 19th Century
This view looks south down the main village street. The road to
Ballymena is to the immediate right behind the lady with the
apron. The premises on both sides of the street are easily
recognised from their modern replacements or renovations. The
number of people here, obviously very intent on the novelty of
a photographer, give an accurate picture of the bustling nature
of the village in this period. The horse and trap may well be on
its way to the Doagh railway station at Ballypallady. The man
with the child in the left foreground is thought to be the
national school master, R. B. Robson.
(W. G. Baird, Belfast; Miss E. Boston Coll.)

COGRY SPINNING MILL, *c.1920*

Workers had no easy task in Cogry spinning mill. Apart from moving close to exposed belts and machinery they were often soaked through lifting the bobbins of rove from troughs of cold water. This cold water spinning process was a distinctive, innovative feature of this mill. The aprons were an ineffective protection from wet and cold. Often the women not only worked in bare feet but travelled to the mill without footwear.

The day began at six o'clock in the morning and, broken only by a few short meal breaks lasted until six o'clock at night. If they were lucky, young workers had the advantage of being 'half - timers 'able to spend part of the day at school and the rest at work. But then of course they had a visit to the Cogry Mill cinema to look forward to in the evenings. (D. Acheson Coll.)

Cheerio! Good Evening
HERE'S GOOD NEWS.

HENDERSON
MOSS ROAD
BALLYCLARE

Has fine Value in
High Class & Up-to-Date
SUITINGS.
And I say he can fit
YOU in correct
CUT and STYLE

GIVE HIM A TRIAL.

HENDERSON'S YOUR MAN

COGRY CINEMA ADVERTISING PLATE
This advertising plate was projected at the cinema built in 1919 at Cogry Mill by the owners, the McMeekin family. It was on a site formerly occupied by a clubroom for workers set up by Ivan McMeekin, the son of the proprietor. It could accommodate about 400 people and had a stage with footlights for variety concerts which were usually held here with the film shows, as part of the evening's programme. A dance floor was also somehow squeezed into the floor space. Club members, generally mill workers, used the hall for the first three days of the week and it was open to the public for the other two. On Saturdays there were two performances to cope with the crowds flocking to Cogry, the only place in the Ballyclare district offering this novel entertainment. The cinema closed in 1932 but the hall has been preserved by the present owner. (Ballyclare & District Historical Society Coll.)

TILDARG

No doubt because of the number of signs on main routes pointing to Tildarg, the name is familiar to many people who would not recognise it if they actually did pass through the principality. It is, in fact, a townland three miles north of Ballyclare bounded by small streams but with no real centre like Ballyeaston or Doagh. At one point, certainly, there is a school and an orange hall and there used to be a pub but this was closed around thirty years ago. In the 19th century it was known as Barclay's Inn when it was the site of important auctions.

Tildarg is derived from an earlier name used in 1609 on the Calendar of the Irish Patent Rolls of James 1. To identify boundaries within the county, the landmark 'the old fort at Tullaghdarge' is mentioned. In Irish this means 'the red outcrop of rock' and such a feature can still be seen close to the ruins of an old fort. This earthworks of banks and ditches, unusual by its size and rectangular shape, was excavated in 1982 as part of the archaeological survey of county Antrim and found to be of considerable interest. On a platform within the enclosure, evidence was found of an unusual medieval house form, and the last use of this was reckoned to have been between the years 1185 and 1375. Then it would have served as a summer base for herdspeople - probably old women and children. The term 'the Tildarg House' is now used to classify this form of house construction and local people are very proud of the distinction.

The area around the Isle Orr river which rises on Drumadarragh Hill overlooking the townland, supported a thriving linen industry for generations. There was at least one bleach green here in the 17th and 18th centuries and a dam and mill have existed at Breckenhill in Tildarg since the 18th century. A 'new dam' beside the spread field was excavated around 1840. Beetling of linen cloth continued on this site until the 1950s and the wheels and machinery remain though their condition is fast deteriorating. Traces of linen can be seen on some rollers. The lower dam is now a trout fishery and attracts a wide variety of wild life, especially birds, to this site of such natural beauty.

As a boy Sir Samuel Ferguson the noted antiquarian and poet, lived for some time in a large house on the slopes of the Collin mountain and it has been recounted how he enjoyed dropping bluebells into the Isle Orr river at Tildarg. The Fergusons traced their ancestry to the Gillians of Collin House and Sir Samuel's popular ballad about the outlawed Covenanter, Willy Gilliland, is about his illustrious ancestor.

In 1946 the Matthews family of Tildarg acquired unusual fame. John Matthews had emigrated to Canada in 1912 from the herd's house where he lived as a gamekeeper for the Dixon estate. His wife Agnes refused to leave Tildarg so her husband set off on his own. He did well and acquired a 320 acre farm in Saskatchewan but, although he had retained no contact with Tildarg, in 1946 he decided to sell up and return. He told no one of his intentions except, perhaps unwisely, a reporter sharing the voyage from Canada. When he reached the docks at Belfast he was met by a posse from the press who had all clearly grasped the news value of the story and escorted him by taxi to his old home. Agnes, completely unaware of her husband's imminent arrival, was tidying up the kitchen when she saw the unusual sight of a taxi at the door. A tall, wiry, old man carrying a Gladstone bag came up the garden path. "Are you Aggie?" he simply asked as she opened the door. "Aye I'm Aggie," she told him. "Well I'm John," he replied and they retreated quietly indoors to take up their lives together again after such a long break. In Belfast, where the story had created a great deal of interest, it became the custom for courting couples meeting to greet each other in the Tildarg fashion. "Are you Aggie? I'm John!" became a catch phrase, so the Matthews couple, in their own peculiar way, contributed to spreading the fame of Tildarg abroad and giving those signposts some meaning to travellers.

AGGIE AND JOHN, AT HOME IN TILDARG, ON THE
DAY OF THE PRODIGAL'S RETURN

L.O.L. 632 TILDARG, *c.*1900

The lodge can be identified from the name on the Lambeg drum and the site of the photograph is just recognisable as a lane beside Tildarg Orange Hall. All efforts to identify anyone in the picture have failed. This fact and the unusual dress of the master of the lodge indicate that this is a very old print. Tildarg

Orange Hall was built in 1875 on land donated by the Delacherois family, prominent local landowners. A silver trowel from the laying of the foundation stone and a long poem celebrating this occasion are still held locally.
(Mrs I. Slane Coll.)

SCHOOL CHILDREN FROM TILDARG, *c.*1912

These children all attended Tildarg National School. This photograph was taken about half a mile from the school in the middle of McClelland's Brae on the Collin Road, the main route from Ballyclare to Broughshane. Some of the large trees still remain on this section of road but it is now a very busy road. There is a modern primary school today in Tildarg catering for children from the wide rural area surrounding the school.

Back row, left to right: Margaret Barr, Anne Semple, Anne Robinson, Anna Gault, Hessie Harvey, Hugh Maybin, Johnny Harvey, Johnny Gault, Tom McClean, Lily Maybin, Margaret McClean.
Front row: Margaret Harvey, Edith Robinson, Leslie McClelland, Agnes Semple. (A. Gault Coll.)

PARKGATE

The village of Parkgate, as its name suggests, is situated on the boundary of the Donegall estate property, right beside one of entrances to this great park. The houses, clustering around the gate, supported the usual range of trades and businesses, catering for the surrounding countryside. Few survive today but the local inn does have a long history. For many years Parkgate supported a busy fair at which a variety of animals were traded. However, Parkgate's most famous fair was held in 1870 and featured an animal not often seen for sale in an open market.This bizarre story all began when some very strange posters appeared in the neighbourhood. In his *History of the Parish of Kilbride* Rev. Roy Cox gives a lively account of Parkgate's famous escapade:

The posters announced that on the 30th June a representative of the Peruvian government would be in attendance at Parkgate, at the hour of eleven in order to purchase cats. As these were required to deal with a plague of mice in Peru, the better cats would fetch the highest prices. Only well fed cats would be purchased. As the news spread everyone became cat conscious. If the señor from Peru was eager to buy cats, he would not be disappointed. For a week or two these humble creatures were kept indoors, many receiving such luxuries as eggs and milk. Just before the great day dawned, the rumour was spread that only cats in suitable containers would be purchased.This led to a demand for potato sprouting boxes which were easily converted into cat cages.

All roads in the district led to Parkgate on that market day. Pony traps, donkey carts and even baby carriages served to transport their valuable load of cats in every sort of container human ingenuity could devise. A most impressive assembly of well-nourished cats was ready and waiting by 10 o'clock, and still they came. The dealers, who had only previously dealt with cattle, horses and pigs, were very active buying and selling cats, and some of them had ready for the señor, quite valuable collections. Zero hour approached and passed but there was no sign of 'the man of the moment'. Even the cats grew impatient for this was not the treatment they were accustomed to of late. Then a sigh of relief and the news went through the crowd that 'He' was coming at last. 'He' had another man with him and there was a large box of money on the back of the carriage. But it was not 'He' only one of the local gentry, Lord Templeton, who had difficulty in threading

his way through that noisy, cat-calling assembly. Cats began to fall in price when 12 o'clock passed by, but excitement mounted once more when another top-hatted figure was seen approaching in haste. This was surely the man they were all waiting for, but no, it was the minister who was curious to know what all the noise was about.

As time wore on, the truth dawned on many that they had been hoaxed. Many angry words were heard as they opened the cat containers and released over a thousand cats, mostly well nourished, on Parkgate. Such is the stuff we are made of, there was much laughter to be heard from many who, seriously out of pocket, made their way back home, minus the treasured animals of a few hours before. And those who knew who was responsible for the hoax kept silent.

However when James McNeice got married some time later, he may have been reminded of the great day, for, as he sat before the fire with his wife on their wedding night, a bagful of cats came down the chimney. These cats released themselves with disastrous results, but no one really let the cat out of the bag.

PARKGATE VILLAGE, *c*.1920

Facing west towards Antrim along the main street, an assortment of farm implements and a cart stand are seen outside the blacksmith's shop, one of two on the village street in this period. The man standing at the door here is the smith, thought to be Jim McAuley. His residence is the tall house next door. The pump remains today and supplied the village water until the well caved in some twenty years ago after a collision. At the end of this row of thatched cottages is the village inn, still there today, single storied but now slated. Further down, past the entry is a drapery shop then the post office and the large detached house is Stirling's grocery shop. Sadly too few of the fine trees remain today. (W. A. Green)

TEMPLEPATRICK, *c*.1920

The view looks west towards Antrim with the Castle Upton estate wall on the right and the Templetown Arms opposite. This was one of a group of inns in the Ulster Public House Trust Company, a body established by the historian F. J. Biggar among others, to reform the drink trade. Its crown and shamrock emblem symbolises the non-sectarian nature of this enterprise. This inn became the Pig and Chicken Roadhouse under the ownership of Cyril Lord, the carpet tycoon, in the 1950s but it was demolished two years ago and a new hotel, the Templeton Inn, built on the site. From this point to Lough Neagh at Antrim, the river continues to pass through the typical Six Mile valley landscape of rich agricultural land and areas of water powered industry but from Templepatrick downstream the people have traditionally looked towards the county town rather than to Ballyclare as a market centre. It therefore seems a suitable place to end the journey along this beautiful river valley. (W. A. Green)

THE PHOTOGRAPHS

Ballyclare is fortunate in having had a series of excellent photographers active in the area since about 1880 and, just as important, others who have preserved their prints. One of the finest was John Cunningham while George McKeown and Robert Grange also built up substantial collections of quality photographs. The former was himself a fine photographer and it is often difficult to distinguish beteeen his own prints and the work of others he collected over the years. This is an easier task with Cunningham's work because many of his plates which George McKeown managed to obtain have the initials J. C. and the date scratched in the corner of the glass. Many people fondly remember the copies of these which were displayed in the window of Jack McClean's chemist's shop in the town square during the May Fair in the 1950s. These survive for posterity.

In addition to the photographs taken by locals, the work of some commercial photographers who occasionally visited the area has also survived. The W. A. Green collection, held in the Ulster Folk and Transport at Cultra, Holywood, contains twenty good quality plates of the Ballyclare district. And, as the many fine photographs which turn up regularly indicate, a visiting photographer took pictures of factory groups in the area during the 1930s. It has not yet been possible to identify the individual or his company's name. Guide books of Ballyclare, too, are a useful source, especially as the photographs they contain often cover the neighbouring villages. However the quality of the few copies which remain, is often poor and good reproduction is therefore difficult.

The photographs in this book were taken in the period from about 1890 to 1941. The quality of some is rather poor but they have been included because these imperfect copies do enable the book to cover a greater variety of life in the valley than if only top quality photographs had been used.

I have tried to use many photographs including people and, where space allows, to identify at least some of the individuals. I believe that our local photographers in the past have been particularly observant and have consistently produced interesting prints. I am confident that their reproduction in this publication will establish their reputation outside the Six Mile valley.

In attributing the photographs in the book a name alone under a print identifies the photographer. The use of the word 'Coll.' after the name simply indicates that the copy is in this person's possession but does not necessarily imply that it forms part of a large set of photographs. Indeed, other than Robert Grange and George McKeown the local collections are quite small.

Ballyclare and District Historical Society is proud of its large archive of historical photographs and is always keen to add to this collection. It is always sad to hear of interesting photographs being thrown away because they have not been considered important enough to be preserved. The society hopes that eventually there will be a site in the centre of Ballyclare where these fine photographs, and the other artefacts it has preserved, can be placed on permanent display.

Acknowledgements

I am grateful to the following for lending me copies of photographs and giving permission for their publication:

The Ulster Folk and Transport Museum (The W. A. Green Collection); The Larne Times; Mr David Acheson; Mr Tom Allan; Mr John Blair; Miss Elizabeth Boston; Mr Jack Boyd; Mr Colin Forde; Mr Leslie Gordon; Mr Jack Grange; Mr. Samuel Graham; Mrs Joan McAdoo; Mr Hamilton McConnell; Mr Bill McFarland; Mrs Winnie Mairs; Miss Eileen Meharg; Dr Bert Millar; Mrs Ruby Nelson; Mrs Roberta Surgeoner; Mr Jimmy Todd.

The following gave me important information regarding the main text or captions for photographs:

Mr Tom Allen; Mr David Boyd; Mr Jimmy Clements; Mr Michael Coulter; Mrs Sylvia Davis; Mr Colin Forde; Mr Samuel Graham; Mr Jack Grange; Mr Knox Greer; Mr Bobby Hayes; Mr David Heaney; Mr David Hill; Mrs Jenny Horner; Mr Hamilton McConnell; Mr Bobby and Mrs Sally McKinstry; Mr Millar Martin; Dr Bert Millar; Mr Alfred Montgomery; Mrs Ruby Nelson; Mr David Nesbitt; Mr Gerald Nutt; Mr Tom and Mrs Renée Peoples; Mr Enrie Scott; Mrs Elizabeth Strange; Mr Jimmy Todd.

I would thank **Mr Ernie Scott** for allowing me to use the first verse of his poem **'The Six Mile Valley'** on the title page.

I am grateful for assistance with word processing from Miss K. Nixon, Mrs J. Glenn, Mrs V. Scott and Mr A. Reid.

Sources

As always, my main source for the information in the book was Robert Grange's unpublished manuscript history of the Ballyclare district.

R. T. Grange 1930-1970 *On the banks of the Ollar*
This fine work, with the memories and tapes of the regular conversations we had in the twelve years before his death, provided me with much of my knowledge of the Six Mile Water valley.

The following books and articles were also consulted:

Brannon, N.F. in *Ulster Journal of Archaeology* Vol. 47. (D.O.E. N.I., Belfast, 1984)

Dubourdieu, Rev. J., *Statistical Survey of the County of Antrim* (Belfast, 1812)

McIlroy, Archibald, 3rd Ed *When lint was in the bell* (Belfast, 1903)

McIlroy, Archibald, *By lone Craig-Linnie Burn* (Belfast, 1900)

McIlroy, Archibald, *The auld Meetin'-Hoose Green* (Belfast, 1898)

McDowell, F. M., *Roses and rainbows* (Belfast, 1974)

McDowell, F.M., *Other days around me* (Belfast, 1966)

Ed. by Bigger, F. J., and Crone, J. S., *Articles and Sketches* (Belfast, 1927)

Cox, Rev. R. R., *A history of the parish of Kilbride* (Kilbride, 1959)

Patterson, E., *The Ballymena Lines* (Newton Abbot, 1968)

McKinney, J., 2nd Ed. *Facts, figures and fractions* (Antrim, 1983)

McKinney, J., *They came in cars and carts* (Antrim, 1989)

Official guide to Ballyclare (London, 1926)

Sketch of a ramble to Antrim by Samuel Miskimmin in *The Belfast Magazine*, (Belfast, May 1809)

Programme for a Bazaar in Ballyclare Presbyterian Church in 1899 (Ballyclare, 1899)

Souvenir programme for Frank Blair's farewell concert in Ballyclare Cinema on Friday 28th November 1930 (Ballyclare, 1930)

The News Letter of 7th April 1739

Finally I would readily acknowledge the assistance I received from so many folk in Ballyclare and the villages of the Six Mile valley far too numerous to mention individually and thank them for their part in supplying facts for this publication.